Celebrating the Law?

Celebrating the Law?

Rethinking Old Testament Ethics

Hetty Lalleman

PATERNOSTER

Paternoster Press is an imprint of Authentic Media,
9 Holdom Avenue, Bletchley, Milton Keynes, MK1 1QR, UK
and Box 1047, Waynesboro, GA 30830-2047, USA
www.authenticmedia.co.uk

British Library Cataloguing in Publication Data

A catalogue record for this book is available from the British
Library
ISBN 1-84227-265-9

Cover Design by 4-9-0 ltd
Print Management by Adare Carwin
Printed and bound by AIT Nørhaven A/S

Contents

Preface

This book began life in my mother tongue, Dutch.[1] It filled a gap in the Old Testament literature on ethics for a lay public and it was well received so that, after I had come to live in England with my family, friends encouraged me to prepare an English version. This was done in the stimulating environment of Spurgeon's College, where I am an associate tutor in Old Testament.

Yet this is no straight translation. I have left out elements that were only relevant in the Dutch situation and have interacted with some of the literature in English which appeared since 1999 when the book was originally published. I hope that this book in its new form will help all Christians, as well as students of theology, gain a better understanding of the subject.

In the preface to the Dutch version I wrote:

Early on in my own life, the Old Testament took an important place. Through my studies I became ever more fascinated by it. The Old Testament is by no means a simple book and it takes time and energy to gain an understanding of it. I hope that the present book will be of some assistance in this respect. My own journey of discovery has not yet come to an end, so I cannot pretend that this book is the final word. I just hope that my readers will become enthusiastic (again) for the Old Testament.

The original Dutch title, translated literally, is Vitally Important. This title expresses my deep conviction that it is important for every Christian, as well as for the church as a whole, to correctly understand Old Testament ethics. This is just as true in the English-speaking world as it is in the Netherlands.

I wish to express my thanks to Professor Gert Kwakkel (Kampen, Netherlands) for his help with the original book and to Arthur Rowe of Spurgeon's College for his help with this version. Both versions have profited greatly from improvements suggested by my husband Pieter.

Hetty Lalleman
London, Spring 2004

Introduction

"The law of the LORD is perfect, reviving the soul" (Ps. 19:7). This is what the author of Psalm 19 tells us, and he continues by using several other words for the "law," such as "statutes," "precepts," "commands" and "ordinances." Each of these words describes the body of prescriptions God gave to his chosen people, Israel. These commands are a source of great joy to the author of the Psalm. They give "joy to the heart" (v. 8), they are "more precious than gold" and "sweeter than honey" (v. 10). God's commandments show the psalmist the right path to follow and prevent him from going astray. Psalm 119, the longest psalm in the Bible, is equally positive about God's rules for life – his law.

People today are not comfortable using such positive language about laws. "Authority" usually has a negative connotation, as does the word "law." Are the precepts and commandments of the Old Testament indeed a source of joy and enthusiasm?

Even evangelical Christians, who confess that the Bible is the authoritative word of God, often have difficulties in understanding the enthusiasm of the Old Testament believers for the law. In theory these Christians do not want to ignore anything from the Bible, but in practice they often do. Large parts of the

Old Testament remain unread, or at best misunderstood. Most believers simply do not read the laws and commands in the first five books of the Bible, putting them aside as irrelevant for everyday life.

Yet at the same time in modern society there is great interest in ethical issues, both inside and outside the church. Questions about norms and values are highly relevant because of radical changes in society. One may ask whether many of the techniques and instruments developed by humankind can legitimately be used or not. Is all that is possible also ethically justified?

What is ethics about? I will not give a philosophical definition because that is not my area of expertise. Put simply, ethics is a reflection on human acts and conduct from the perspective of good and evil. In the study of ethics we ask questions such as: What are we allowed or not allowed to do? What should we do in particular situations and what should we not do? What is the right way to act? These issues are relevant not only to scholars, but to "lay people" as well, since we all need to make these decisions every day.

God calls the Christian community to think through all decisions from a biblical perspective. There are Christian professionals who are doing much good work in this area, such as the London Institute for Contemporary Christianity (http//www.licc.org.uk), the Jubilee Centre in Cambridge (http://www.jubilee-centre.org/), the Whitefield Institute in Oxford (http://www.whitefield-institute.org.uk/), and the Center for Applied Christian Ethics at Wheaton College (www.wheaton.edu/CACE). There are specialized organizations like the Christian Medical Fellowship (http://www.cmf.org.uk/) and the Center for Bioethics and Human Dignity (www.cbhd.org), which deal (among other things) with ethical decisions in the medical area. But "ordinary" believers, too, need a framework for Christian ethics. The general public accepts many activities that were not acceptable in the past. How is the Christian to act in a world that increasingly ignores, or even rejects, biblical values?

This book seeks to explain how Christians can use the Old Testament to make sense of ethical issues. We will try to listen carefully to the Bible. My approach will be not to discuss individual biblical texts on specific topics or "hot items." Rather, I will try to provide some general principles. The societies in which the people of God in the Old and New Testaments lived were very similar to the world in which the Christian church in the West has lived since World War II. The people of God live in a world which is alienated from God. The people of Israel were a minority in the Old Testament world, as was the New Testament church in its day. Just like us, they lived in what is now called a "multi-religious" and "multi-cultural" society. God gave his people his "rules for living," his "signposts," in a world like that. This book looks at those "signposts" in the context of our world today.

The Ten Commandments

When people consult the Bible on ethical issues, they often refer immediately to the Ten Commandments. Many Christians consider the Decalogue to be an exception to the complicated question concerning which Old Testament commands we need to obey and which ones we can disregard, because nearly everybody considers them to be relevant for all times. Their influence and relevance reach beyond the church, for many Western legal systems are rooted in the social rules of the Ten Commandments. Everybody agrees that "Thou shalt not kill" continues to be a fundamental rule for society, even though different people interpret the rule in different ways. But, apart from the Ten Commandments, many of the Old Testament commands are neither read nor understood. In this book I want to focus on some of those passages that are less self-evident.

The commandments in the Old Testament are mainly found in the first five books of the Bible, which together are called the Torah in Hebrew and the Pentateuch in Greek. However, these books contain many stories as well. Most people greatly appreciate these stories – reading them, listening to them or even watching modern versions of the stories on television or video. Yet the same people who read the stories of Abraham and Moses in the books of Genesis and Exodus, for example, consider the "laws" in the same books to be more or less an embarrassment. I have met many people who have told me that they consider the Torah to be a sort of "law book" which, for the most part, they do not need to read.

A note about the word "Torah" might be useful. This word is often translated "law." The Old Testament was thus divided into the Law, Historical Books, Prophets, and Poetical Books (or, following the Jewish division, into Law, Prophets, and Writings). "Law," however, is not the best translation of "Torah." In the first place, the first five books of the Bible contain not only laws but also large amounts of narrative material. In the second place, the word "law" is too much associated with police officers and courts of law. A more adequate translation is "teaching" or "directions for life." This is what the Jewish writer Martin Buber tried to emphasize, making up a German word "Weisung," to describe it: the Torah points us in a certain direction, showing and explaining how believers can live their lives in the way God wants them to. In Hebrew, the Ten Commandments (in Greek, "the Decalogue") are called "the Ten Words" – which sounds less didactic than our "commandments." Humans instinctively dislike the idea of a higher authority, of revealed commands.

Christ

Christians may have another reason for not seriously considering the laws in the Old Testament – and this barrier is a theological one: has the law not been abolished because of what Jesus did on the cross? A Christian has been brought into a living relationship with God by grace, and not by works of the law (cf. Rom. 3:21–24; Eph. 2:8–9). Through grace we are declared "righteous." No "good works" will ever add anything substantial to that fact. And is that not exactly what the Old Testament laws are about – doing "good works"? If that is indeed the case, then laws belong to the past since Jesus came to earth and saved us through grace.

The problem is clear. In order to understand more of the joy of the law about which the Israelite would sing, as in Psalms 19 and 119, we need to lay aside our presuppositions about the Old Testament. We need to discover the value of the laws in Old Testament times and how modern people can learn from them. This is a major challenge. How can these old laws be relevant, let alone be applied, today?

My first concern here is the Christian church. How relevant the biblical laws are for the world outside the church is a matter of debate and depends on one's view of the relationship between church and state. Christians differ widely in their opinions on this matter, but my chief concern in this book will be to stimulate thinking about the relevance of Old Testament ethics for Christians themselves.

I am a Christian writing from a Christian perspective. My concern is that evangelical Christians should no longer regard the Old Testament, and in particular the legal parts of the Torah, as "out of date." In order to rethink our position here, we need to understand these passages in context. This means that readers must try to set aside their presuppositions and be open to listen to the word in the world of the Old Testament.

This book does not contain *the* Old Testament ethics. It would be impossible to try to offer such an ethics because the Bible is not a systematic "handbook of ethics." Since ethics has to do with the dynamics of human life in this world, it is important for Christians to think about and study what the Old Testament tells us about the sort of attitudes and conduct God expects from his people.

Recent German and Dutch literature has not paid much attention to the ethical relevance of the Old Testament, often focusing solely on exegetical problems in parts of the Torah. More studies on ethical issues have been published in the English-speaking world, reflecting a greater awareness of the political and practical implications of faith. In what follows we will discuss and evaluate some of this literature. The purpose of the present book is to give a more general framework for thinking about ethics, instead of focusing on specific issues.

About this book

The first chapter presents a brief survey and analysis of how the church and some of its theologians have tried to fit Old Testament ethics into their thinking. This material provides a basis for further exploration in the following chapters.

The second chapter investigates the historical and theological features of the Old Testament. As we shall see, creation and covenant are very important issues since they contribute to a better understanding of Old Testament laws and commands.

In Chapter 3, a discussion of the work of some scholars who have written on the subject provides a basis for formulating a framework of some basic characteristics of ethics in the Old Testament. In Chapters 4 through 6, then, we test this framework by taking some specific examples of Old Testament laws and studying them with this "model." Some thorough exegesis is of great importance here. Chapter 7, finally, establishes connections between the passages dealt with and Jesus Christ and the New Testament church. Each chapter concludes with some questions for reflection or discussion.

1

Approaching the Old Testament

Three ways

We saw in the Introduction that the function of laws in the Old Testament, apart from the Ten Commandments, remains something of a mystery for Christians.

Throughout the ages, the church has tried to find ways to use the commands and laws of the Old Testament. Church leaders have often divided the material according to the areas to which the laws relate. In the time of the Reformation, for example, the Reformers distinguished the following three ways of using the Torah:

1. *usus politicus* or *usus civilis*: the law is supposed to restrict sin and to promote justice. Not denying any other uses, the law is meant to have a key role in public life and politics.
2. *usus elenchticus* or *usus pedagogicus*: the law is there to make humans aware of their sins in order to lead them to Christ for salvation.
3. *usus didacticus* or *usus normativus*, also called *tertius usus legis* ("the third use of the law"): the law is given to provide believers with a norm for their lives, as a "light on their path."[2]

Martin Luther and his followers emphasized the second use of the law. According to them, the laws of the Old Testament were intended to convict people of their guilt before God. In this way the law had prepared the way for the coming of Christ. They did not pay much attention to the third use of the law, because they stressed the fact that a Christian is no longer "under the law." In his catechisms, however, Luther built on the Ten Commandments.[3] Luther's followers seem to be more consistent in contrasting the Old and the New Testament than he himself probably intended. Luther's contrast between "law" and "promise," or "grace" (Old versus New Testaments) is still very influential today.

John Calvin took a different approach by defending the first and the third functions of the law. He declared many more elements of the legal sections of the Old Testament valid for the church than just the Ten Commandments. God's rules give directions for life on earth in the present world as well, Calvin argues. His view of the law was much more positive than Luther's. He softened Luther's contrast between the Old and the New Testaments and argued that the covenant with Abraham extends to the New Testament period and to the Christian church.

A rather radical group of Calvinists today advocates what is called "Theonomism." With an appeal to Calvin, they declare that the Old Testament law applies not only to Christians, but to all people in a state as well. This group also calls itself "Christian Reconstructionists" because they want to reshape society towards a theocracy according to the laws in the Old Testament. Their movement is strongest in the United States, where they want the death penalty to become law throughout the country. Leading representatives are Rousas Rushdoony, Greg Bahnsen and Gary North. We may legitimately ask whether this modern position is really what Calvin had in mind.[4]

Dispensationalism

A radical contrast with the Calvinist ideas of broad application of the Old Testament law is found in J. N. Darby and many Dispensationalists after him. They think that Israel and the church represent two completely separate "dispensations," which have very little in common. According to this view, the Old Testament legislation is irrelevant to Christians in practical issues. Strict Dispensationalists see the Old Testament's relevance for the Christian church only in its typological or allegorical use.

Darby had strong convictions about the contrast between the Old and the New Testaments, which we can clearly see in the following statement:

> The Father reveals himself to our souls by the gospel, by the Spirit of adoption; but Jehovah makes himself known by his Judgments, by the exercise of his power on the earth. . . . The Jews then are the people by whom, and in whom, God sustains his name of Jehovah, and his character of judgement and righteousness. The Church are the people in whom, as in his family, the Father reveals his character of goodness and love.[5]

Darby contrasts the character of the God of the Old Testament with that of the God of the New Testament. He does this by using different names ("Jehovah" versus "Father") and contrasting attributes like "judgement" and "love."[6] Such a distinction between the Old and the New Testaments, however, is untenable in the light of a more careful reading of both. Is Hosea 11 not a great example of God's love for Israel? And does Jesus, on the other hand, not frequently speak about judgement? What about the following words from the letter to the Hebrews: "for our 'God is a consuming fire'" (12:29)? The author of Hebrews here quotes deliberately from the Old Testament (Deut. 4:24). Besides, Jesus taught his own disciples, who could not yet be considered "Christians," to call God their "Father."

It is not the purpose of this book to deal with the rather extreme position of Darby and Dispensationalism at any length. It is important, however, to be aware of the inconsistencies in the logical conclusion of this position, because many Christians today operate with the same contrast at the back of their minds – often without realizing it. They mistakenly assume that the Old Testament is about "law" while the New is about "grace."

Historical-critical research

The above opinions on the use of the Torah have all resulted from a certain doctrinal approach. Modern biblical scholarship deals differently with the Old Testament. In the historical-critical research which has flourished since the Enlightenment, scholars have tried to discover the origins and the history of tradition of the Torah. Scholars have studied and analyzed the laws and commandments and offered many different hypotheses concerning their origin, development, and application – nearly all of which deny the Mosaic authorship of the laws, which the Old Testament itself claims. Historical-critical research usually distinguishes several layers in the texts as we have them today, and scholars identify

these layers as originating from different times and circumstances. Gerhard von Rad developed the idea of
different traditions within the "Hexateuch" (Genesis–
Joshua) and identified stories that developed around
themes such as the exodus. The core of the different traditions is the "short historical creed" he found in
Deuteronomy 26: "A wandering Aramean was my
father . . .," which sums up the most important stages in
Israel's history. The historical-critical consensus is that
the different traditions were connected at a later stage
and, in this way, the Old Testament was shaped over
many centuries.[7]

Such analysis frequently resulted in attributing more
theological relevance to some layers than to others. The
unspoken presupposition is often that older texts have
more relevance for the church of today. A clear example
of this approach is Claus Westermann, who distinguishes between "commandments" and "laws."
Commandments have the form of "Thou shalt not"
(think of the Ten Commandments), whereas "laws" are
the longer regulations about issues such as slavery.
Westermann draws a wide-ranging conclusion from this
formal distinction:

> In the Sinai narrative, only the Decalogue in Exodus 20 is
> the word of God coming to Israel from the divine moun-
> tain. The Covenant Code, which originated separately from
> it after the land acquisition (Exod. 21–23), was added
> subsequently. . . . The commandments are direct and imme-
> diate words of God as address, and have their place in wor-
> ship. The law is tied to human institutions . . .[8]

We see that, in this view, commandments and laws have
a different theological relevance. As Westermann says,
"It was only subsequently, at a later stage, that the laws

were explained as God's word."[9] Therefore Westermann thinks it is perfectly legitimate for the Christian church to uphold the Ten Commandments but to consider the other rules as far less relevant – if they are relevant at all. In this way he draws conclusions from what is, after all, a mixture of historical research and his own presuppositions.

According to Theodorus Christiaan Vriezen, the fact that the Old Testament canon was accepted by the Jews as it is now should not bind the church to its contents. He expresses difficulties with accepting as God's revelation

> . . . certain parts of the Law (the ritual parts) and of the historical books (certain parts of the stories of Jacob and Samson) . . . Here and there other parts could be found in which the Christian can only with great difficulty (or not at all) find the revelation of the Spirit of God, but rather the revelation of the spirit of the age (Ecclesiastes) or of the spirit of the Jewish people (Ps. cxxxvii, Esther).

Vriezen further postulates that many parts of the Old Testament may be beautiful literature, like Ecclesiastes, "but one cannot call them a message, a revelation of God, or find in them a trace of that activity of the Holy Spirit which was revealed in Jesus Christ."[10]

Alternative approaches

In biblical research today, the "old" hypotheses of the historical-critical research, which distinguished literary sources behind the Pentateuch, no longer receive general support. Opinions now differ widely on the origins, contents, and dating of any sources. In particular, there is a wide variety of scholarly opinions with regard to the hypothetical sources J and E.[11] About thirty years ago, scholars dated J to the tenth century BC, but today some would date it to the exilic (or even as late as the postexilic) period. Many doubt whether E was a distinct source for Genesis at all.

With so many different opinions on the origins of the Pentateuch, it seems unwise to evaluate the laws based on when or how they originated. Two other scholarly methods for dealing with the Old Testament would seem to be more fruitful.

Firstly, some argue the merits of studying the Old (and the New) Testaments in their present form, namely as (parts of) the canon of the Christian church. Historical issues and problems should not keep us from appreciating the Bible as the book that was accepted as a unity by the church; therefore the book is theologically relevant as a whole. Its theological value could not possibly depend on prevailing theories and hypotheses about the origin of the text, as if these determined the meaning of the text. Scholars who represent this "canonical approach"[12] focus on the way in which each passage has been interpreted within the traditions of the synagogue and of the Christian church. These scholars also look at how each passage relates to the whole of the Scriptures.

Other scholars approach the Old Testament text from a more literary perspective, treating each passage as a rather timeless unity in itself. They try to discover the structure of a text or of a whole Bible book and search for smaller units within. In so doing they pay attention to such details as the repetition of words and try to determine the function of such repetition. They do not consider repetitions as superfluous or as proof of the involvement of different authors, as historical-critical scholars would do. Concentric structures are also important in this literary approach.[13] A given passage is read as one unity, as a literary unit which has its own meaning and wordplay. Important in the literary approach is also the fact that the text is read and re-read, asking questions such as: What does the text do to me as a reader? What is the author or redactor trying to convey by writing this text in exactly this way? Scholars here assign a greater importance to the "language" of the text itself than to its (hypothetical) origin.

Although the question of how a text originated may be interesting to some, dealing with such historical-critical issues could hinder us from giving full consideration to the texts as they are in the context in which we have them. That context is very important: we have not been given separate sources E or J which we might put together. What we have is the text of the Old Testament as the canon accepted by the Christian church. I am glad this literary approach has been gaining support in recent years. The Heidelberg Old Testament scholar Rolf Rendtorff clearly expresses this return to common sense:

> . . . the exegetical task is not to reconstruct earlier levels that always will remain hypothetical and dependent on the respective methodological approach of the interpreter. Rather exegetes have to try to understand the biblical text in its given form and shape.[14]

Although Rendtorff works with the hypothesis of several "layers" in the Pentateuch, he is convinced that this theory should not receive too much emphasis in the interpretation of the text.

The Canonical-theological approach

As Rendtorff argues, it is important to try to understand the text of the Old Testament laws in its present form. I therefore suggest a "canonical-theological" reading of the Bible. This means, contrary to Westermann, making no theological difference between the various commandments. Rather, the "rules" in the Old Testament are all part of the one Torah.

The New Testament makes clear that "the Law and the Prophets" were Jesus' Bible, the word according to which he lived. The Old Testament plays a very important part in the story of Jesus' temptation by the devil in Matthew 4: Jesus quotes from the book of Deuteronomy. At other moments in his life, and even on the cross, we see how this book – the Old Testament, as such – was of great importance to him.

In the pages that follow we will try to sketch a theological framework for Old Testament ethics. This does not mean starting with today's issues, looking for answers in the Bible. Instead, we will study some key issues in the Old Testament and draw up some general guidelines that each reader may apply to different situations. This book is written from the point of view of the Old Testament and not that of modern ethics. The reader should not expect lists of "what is allowed and what isn't." Old Testament ethics is far more than a collection of rules.

The main question, therefore, is this: How can we find some sort of "system" for dealing with the many different sorts of commandments found in the Old Testament? Can we place them in an overarching theological framework? To be able to answer this question we must discover what these laws tell us about the relationship between God and Israel, and what they say about God's relationship to the world as a whole. What role did the commandments and prescriptions play in the Old Testament and in the history of Israel? As we shall see, there are indeed theological features that can help us in understanding and applying the Old Testament to our lives.

We will concentrate on those parts of the Old Testament which mainly contain laws – the Torah. That does not mean, however, that ethics in the Old Testament is only about laws and regulations.[15]

Questions for further reflection

1. What role (if any) does the Old Testament play in your life?
2. We have looked at three traditional views on the use and function of the laws. What are some strengths and weaknesses of each?
3. Do you think a Christian could do without the Old Testament? Why or why not?

2

In Search of God's Purpose in the Old Testament

Before thinking in more detail about the many commandments in the Torah, it is important to have an overview of what the Old Testament as a whole is about. Biblical scholars have searched for a theological core in the Old Testament, trying to see whether all the stories, laws, prophetic material, and poetic texts can be put under one umbrella. Is the heart of the Old Testament found in the covenant?[16] Or is it God's design[17] or another major theme?

The German scholar Gerhard von Rad stated that there is no central point, no core, in the Old Testament. There are simply different narrative complexes – for instance, the one about the exodus – that together make up the Old Testament.[18] According to von Rad, "theology of the Old Testament," the discipline that studies major themes in the Old Testament, should not focus on one central point to which other themes relate, but should rather concentrate on all of those diverse narrative complexes.

It is not easy to find the core of the Old Testament. The only acceptable core may be "God," for he is there throughout history. This identification of a core does not bring us much further, however, for we must at least

deal with God's diverse *acts* as well as with the revelation of his *being*. The Old Testament does not provide an
abstract theory of "God."

The exodus as the core?

For a long time, the historical-critical approach identified the exodus as the core of Old Testament history, and
it was therefore considered to be at the heart of Old
Testament theology. Historical-critical scholars regarded
the exodus as the beginning of Israel's history and said
that, on that occasion, the faith in one God was first
explicitly stated. At that time Israel became God's people. The accounts of the deliverance from Egypt and of
the covenant at Sinai were considered more important
for Israel's faith than the creation account. Such critical
scholars held that only in and after the Babylonian exile
did Israel begin to confess her faith in God as Creator,
when they were confronted with the religious texts and
gods of Babylon.

This particular view of the origin of the first chapters
of Genesis influenced the way in which the historical-
critical scholars conceived a theology of the Old
Testament. Historical-critical research attributed Genesis
1 to source P, the priestly source, allegedly the "theo-
logian" among the writers of the Pentateuch. But
because this source was considered rather late, the sup-
posedly earlier sources were often given priority in
establishing the theological heart of the Old Testament:
the exodus became more important than creation.

Earlier in this chapter we already came across the fact
that normative conclusions are often drawn from historical-critical research. However, in the canon as we have
it now, the Old Testament does not start with the exodus,

but with creation. We should at least look at the theological relevance of Israel's belief in God as Creator.

Creation

Westermann, who was a student of von Rad, paid more attention to creation than was usual at his time.[19] The crucial theme of creation requires more attention in a theology than even he allowed it, however. When we study the books which now make up our canon of the Bible, it becomes clear that the creation of the world is not important only because of the chronological order in which things happened. Creation also has great theological relevance as the foundation and the essential starting point of the whole Bible, which starts with creation and finishes with re-creation. The history of humankind, of Israel, and of the church is embedded in a universal framework. God's plans reach out to the whole of heaven and earth. God only focuses on "Israel-alone" for a certain period and with a specific purpose. The pivot in world history is God's Kingship; he rules over all he has created. His sovereignty is essential throughout both the Old and New Testaments. We therefore need to investigate and understand the issue of God's Kingship.

Christ

Before we deal with God's Kingship, we return briefly to the question of the core of the Old Testament. Is creation the core? I would not agree with that position either. In fact, every theology of the Old Testament that focuses on one issue is inherently flawed. We cannot emphasize one particular topic and say that others are irrelevant. It is more faithful to the Scriptures as a whole to balance the different elements of the Old Testament without calling one of them "the" core.

Is the quest for a core in the Old Testament in fact a helpful question for Christians at all? H. J. Hermisson highlights the fact that when Christians speak about the "Old" Testament, they already indicate that they look at it from a Christian perspective. He argues that Christians may freely admit that, for them, Christ is the "external" core of the Old Testament. "External," because he is not explicitly mentioned in the Old Testament. Yet Christians read the whole Bible with Christ in mind. According to Hermisson, "God and Israel" is the "internal" core of the Old Testament.[20] This statement is worth considering, although we should be careful not to read Christ into Old Testament texts too quickly.

God's Kingship

In the first chapter of Genesis we read how God works through his mighty word, by which he creates the world. The way in which Genesis 1 describes how God speaks his words has a "royal" connotation: these words sound like "royal decrees." Things that may amaze us every day on earth come into existence because of God's speaking, without the use of any physical power. "Let there be light – and there was light."

The part of Genesis that deals with creation is brief, consisting only of two chapters. The opening chapters of Genesis do not spell out the implications of the fact that God is the Creator. Neither is the idea of God's Kingship elaborated in Genesis as it is in other parts of the Old Testament, such as in the Psalms and the Prophets.

In the Psalms, Israel's "hymnbook," we frequently read about God as the Creator. This theme is related to that of his Kingship. For example, Psalm 24:1–2 says:

> The earth is the LORD's, and everything in it,
> the world, and all who live in it;
> for he founded it upon the seas
> and established it upon the waters.

In the same psalm, verses 7–8, God is welcomed as the King:

> Lift up your heads, O you gates;
> be lifted up, you ancient doors,
> that the King of glory may come in.
> Who is this King of glory?
> The LORD strong and mighty,
> the LORD mighty in battle.

Another example is Psalm 95:3–5:

> For the LORD is the great God,
> the great King above all gods.
> In his hand are the depths of the earth,
> and the mountain peaks belong to him.
> The sea is his, for he made it,
> and his hands formed the dry land.

In God's creative work we see the revelation of his glory, as we read in Psalm 19:1: "The heavens declare the glory of God . . ." The word "majesty" is appropriate here, because it shows the beauty and the royal character of creation. In the same way we read in Psalm 96:5, 6 and 10:

> . . . but the LORD made the heavens.
> Splendor and majesty are before him;

strength and glory are in his sanctuary. . . .
Say among the nations, "The LORD reigns."
The world is firmly established, it cannot be moved;
he will judge the peoples with equity.

We also find confessions of God as the Creator and King in the prophetic books. For example, Jeremiah 10 declares:

But the LORD is the true God;
he is the living God, the eternal King. . . .
But God made the earth by his power;
he founded the world by his wisdom
and stretched out the heavens by his understanding. . . .
for he is the Maker of all things. (vv. 10, 12, 16)

In Isaiah 43:15 we read: "I am the LORD, your Holy One, Israel's Creator, your King." The context of this verse reminds us of God's holiness, his creative and redemptive work, and his Kingship – a complete theology in a few brief lines.

God the Creator and King will also judge the nations, for he is Lord over all. To his people Israel, this confession implies that God is greater than all the gods and rulers of the other nations surrounding them. His people can therefore be saved from the power of the enemies who don't relate to God at all.

We see the theme of God's Kingship carry through from the beginning of the Bible to the very last book. The songs in the book of Revelation praise God's Kingship as he ultimately triumphs over the enemies of God's children. In Revelation 14:7, for example, an angel cries out: "Fear God and give him glory, because the hour of his judgment has come. Worship him who made the heavens, the earth, the sea and the springs of water."[21]

This verse praises God for being a just Judge as well as the Creator.

Image of the King

Psalm 8 is a song about creation that connects the Kingship of God with human beings. They are "crowned . . . with glory and honor" (v. 5), created to be "ruler over the works of your hands; you put everything under his feet" (v. 6). These words are "royal," drawing upon the language normally used with respect to kings. We also have pictures from Egypt of pharaohs seated on their thrones with their feet on footstools, under which lay their enemies. In the Bible, however, humans do not achieve kingship in battle. Rather, God confers it on them. Neither is human kingship about us ruling over other people with power and might. God gives us the responsibility to protect and care for the earth and the animal world. The royal status of human beings is not a right that we deserve. It is given to us. Furthermore, it is a subordinate kingship: humans are "a little lower than the heavenly beings" – they are not divine (Ps. 8:5). The one and only King is God and the kingship each person has, according to Psalm 8, is derived from God's Kingship. Even an earthly king is never "a god on earth" or divine. Earthly kings are to do justice on earth in the way God wants them to.

The role of humans described in Psalm 8 is very different from the role the Babylonians ascribed to them. According to *Enuma Elish*, the Babylonian creation myth, the earth and human beings were created out of chaos. They continued to need protection against the chaos throughout the ages. A good structure in society, in particular through the building and fortification of the city of Babylon, afforded this protection. The king was the "god-king," the vice-regent of the god. In contrast, Psalm 8 sees every human as a "vice-regent of God" who can rule over God's creation according to his decree.[22]

Psalm 24 likewise connects ethics and creation. Between the verses about God's Kingship and those about his creative work cited above we read about ethical conduct:

> Who may ascend the hill of the LORD?
> Who may stand in his holy place?
> He who has clean hands and a pure heart,
> who does not lift up his soul to an idol
> or swear by what is false.
> He will receive blessing from the LORD
> and vindication from God his Savior. (vv. 3–5)[23]

As the King's representatives on earth, human beings may rule over his creation. This psalm reminds us of the words of Genesis 1. It is through God's word that things are created. In Genesis 1:26 and following we read about the creation of man and woman, who are said to be made "in the image of God."

Opinions differ widely on the meaning of "image."[24] One of the possible meanings is that humans represent God on earth. In the ancient Near East, as we have seen with Babylon, kings were regarded as representatives of their gods on earth. In certain locations a god could be represented by his image. Kings could likewise be represented by their image in areas where they themselves were absent.

In the Bible, every human being is meant to represent God on earth. Men and women are "crowned . . . with glory and honor," as we read in Psalm 8. God gave man and woman a decree when he created them: ". . . fill the earth and subdue it. Rule over the fish of the sea and the birds of the air and over every living creature that moves on the ground" (Gen. 1:28). Gordon J. Wenham remarks with regard to the *function* of creation in the image of God:

> . . . it enables mankind to rule over the earth and the other creatures. In ancient oriental myth kings were made in the gods' image, but Genesis democratises the idea; every human being is a king and responsible for managing the world on God's behalf.[25]

Human beings are intended to be God's "vice-regents" on earth – visible representatives of the invisible God. The Bible begins, therefore, with a high estimation of humankind as it sets out a mission statement for human beings.

However we may define the "image of God," there is a link between the image and the task of humankind on earth. Each human being possesses "something" that connects him or her with God. We bear God's "seal" and can deny or affirm this in our lives. In the Old Testament, the fact that all humans are created in the image of God is a key foundation of ethics. God created everyone. On this basis Genesis 9:6 can state that whenever someone kills another being, he kills the image of God. Therefore murder is punished very severely (see also Prov. 14:31). The fact that every other being is created in the image of God is the basis of human rights.

Responsibility in relations

As "representatives" of God, human beings have a great responsibility. The purpose and meaning of life is not "to do nothing" or to have a sort of eternal holiday. Such was the ideal of the Greeks. But, from the very beginning, even *before* Adam and Eve had sinned, they were given some concrete tasks: to rule over the animals (Gen.1:26; 2:19), to have children and raise them (1:28), to subdue the earth (1:28) and to work it (2:5, 15). The responsibilities for children and work did not begin with the curse after the fall in Genesis 3:16–19. The curse simply resulted in these tasks being much heavier than they had originally been intended.

It is important to notice that, even after the fall, humans still derive their value from being created in God's image – neither has God been dethroned as the King of the whole universe. Human life has a purpose and a meaning in that we are representatives of God on earth.

The first chapters of Genesis make clear that human beings live in several relationships: they are related to God, to each other and to the land (the earth, the soil). The influence of sin can be seen in each of these relationships: with God (Gen. 3), with others ("my brother and sister," Gen. 4), and with the earth and the rest of creation. This interconnectedness becomes very clear when Adam and Eve sin: their relationship with God is harmed, their son kills his brother, the cultivation of the land becomes heavy and frustrating (Gen. 3:17–19).

The land plays a significant role in the history of Israel; because of sin the Israelites had to wait to possess the land and even lost it temporarily. We will see later that the commandments of the Old Testament relate to these three key areas: our relationship with God, with other people and with the world (land, the animal world, and even trees).

Creation and history

In the first chapters of Genesis we see that the confession of God as the Creator lays the foundation for what follows in the rest of the Bible. Closely related to his position as the Creator is God's Kingship, and the kingship of humans derived from it. It is important, therefore, not to begin a discussion of the ethics of the Old Testament with Moses or even with Abraham, but with Genesis 1:1.

Genesis 1–11 lay the foundation upon which the biblical story unfolds and develops. These first eleven chapters are about the whole of creation, the origins of all nations. They set the scene for God's history with humankind.[26]

The Bible begins with creation and ends with the re-creation of heaven and earth. The Old Testament is not just about Israel – God has plans for the whole of creation, as we will see more fully below. The Christian faith, likewise, is not just about "God and my soul" or about the small group of followers of Jesus Christ, but about God's kingdom and his purposes for the whole world and the whole of creation.

Another important aspect of the account of creation is that it shows that, from the beginning, God wanted to have a relationship with human beings. When the relationship was distorted by sin he wanted to restore it. God's redemptive activity does not begin with the exodus as has often been thought, but much earlier. Immediately after the fall, God announced his plan of salvation for the world.[27] God protects Adam and Eve from the problems they would have had if – after eating from the tree of life – they had remained in the state of sin forever.

Even in the story of Noah there is the element of grace and redemption in that a remnant is saved from the flood. In Genesis 6:6–7 there is a clear reference to the story of creation in Genesis 1: "The LORD was grieved that he had made man on the earth." Despite this fact there is redemption: Noah "found favor in the eyes of the LORD" (v. 8; the same expression is later used of Moses in Exod. 33:17). Noah is said to be "righteous" and "blameless" (Gen. 6:9). The Bible generally uses such words to describe Israelites who live according to God's commandments. For example, Luke 1:6 describes Zechariah and Elizabeth as follows: "Both of them were upright in the sight of God, observing all the Lord's commandments and regulations blamelessly."

After God rescued Noah and his family, God gave them a new start, which again reminds us of the creation story. God told Noah: "Be fruitful and increase in number and fill the earth" (Gen. 9:1). Yet the same chapter shows that Noah falls into the trap of sinning just as Adam did (Gen. 9:18–23). The result, again, is a curse (vv. 25–27).

In the chapters of Genesis that follow we learn how the nations developed and how they wanted to build a tower to express their unity and power, which they found in themselves and not in God. They were self-seeking, which is the essence of sin. They wanted to "make a name" for themselves (Gen. 11:4). Yet God destroyed their plans and scattered them over all the earth (Gen. 11:8). The consequence of their sin, therefore, was the direct opposite of what they had wished. They were anxious to build a society without the God of heaven and earth, with humankind in complete control. God's response was to spread them and so make an end to their selfishness and arrogance.[28]

The next chapter (Gen. 12) relates how God chooses one man, Abraham, and makes a fresh start with him. "I will make your name great," God says (Gen. 12:2), which is in sharp and conscious contrast with the effort of the humans in the previous chapter to make their own names great. Whereas the nations were scattered in Genesis 11, the nations will be gathered around Abraham – not because of their own initiative, but because of God's. Again the power that drives the story on is God's initiative, his rule, and his Kingship. Through Abraham, God will show what it means that he is the Creator and the King over all the earth. Only by recognizing God for who he is will human beings reach the purpose God set out for them.

The call of Abraham clearly has a universal goal: *all* nations will share in his blessing. God has chosen to create a specific place on earth where his ideal reign will be visible, and in the Old Testament that place is the land of Israel. But God promised Abraham right from the start that the whole earth would be blessed through the nation of Israel, ". . . and all peoples on earth will be blessed through you" (Gen. 12:3).

It is evident throughout the book of Genesis that God wants to rescue people and to have a relationship with them. He confirms this objective by entering into covenants with Abraham. On various difficult occasions he assures the patriarchs Isaac and Jacob of his saving presence. The story of Joseph in particular demonstrates how the future of God's people is reassured. Redemption starts long before the events of the exodus.[29]

One nation as an example

At first view it seems that, from chapter 12 onwards, the book of Genesis focuses on just one nation – the descendants of Abraham – but this is not the case. Although Abraham is the central figure in God's plans,

God is certainly not excluding other nations. All nations on earth will be blessed through Abraham and the nation that consists of his descendants. At the end of Genesis the promises to Abraham have only been partially fulfilled: there are many descendants and, indeed, there is blessing through the lives of the patriarchs. Yet God's people do not live in the promised land. And the question remains: who exactly are "God's people"?

The Old Testament books that follow develop these themes. God rescues his people from slavery and enters into a relationship with them through Moses – a relationship that develops throughout the other books of the Pentateuch. We see how God wants to use his people Israel, the descendants of Abraham, as a kind of "model" for the rest of the world. In the commandments and laws of the Torah we discover what sort of life God wants people to live. Both in its stories and in its laws the Torah shows how God wants to relate to people as well as how God wants people to relate to him and to each other. The laws and commands show us what a life with God as King looks like. In such a life and in a land where people live according to God's will, there will be justice and mercy; God's presence will permeate everything. The other nations should see this difference and be attracted to the one God and Creator. Israel's example should draw others to follow God and his rules as well. Moses expresses the uniqueness of Israel and its commandments, and the effect they may have on other nations:

> Observe them [the decrees and laws taught by Moses] carefully, for this will show your wisdom and understanding to the nations, who will hear about all these decrees and say, "Surely this great nation is a wise and understanding

people." . . . And what other nation is so great as to have such righteous decrees and laws as this body of laws I am setting before you today? (Deut. 4:6, 8)

Israel is a *pars pro toto*, a part which represents the whole: in this land and among this people God's Kingship, which is a Kingship over all the earth, must become visible and effective. This aim is clear from the words Moses is commanded to speak to the people of Israel when God makes a treaty with them:

Now if you obey me [God] fully and keep my covenant, then out of all nations you will be my treasured possession. Although the whole earth is mine, you will be for me a kingdom of priests and a holy nation. (Exod. 19:5–6)

Israel is distinct and should be dedicated to God alone, the King of heaven and earth. The purpose of this unique position is entirely positive. Israel is to represent God for everyone on earth; the people are to be a light to the world.

The Old Testament is full of stories that illustrate the failures of human beings trying to live according to God's rules. It also contains many stories about kingdoms that tried to undermine God's kingdom. Individual rulers often reacted against God, both inside and outside Israel. All sorts of idolatry, which denied the uniqueness of the God of Israel, constantly threatened the recognition of God's rule in Israel. But, despite all this, the ideal of Old Testament ethics is clear and "God's ideal world" is revealed in the commandments he has given. His people were meant to live out the ideal and thus to be a "model," an "example" for other nations. We will return to this concept in the following chapters.

God's Kingship in the New Testament

God's Kingship is a central theme in the New Testament as well. The Gospels often speak about the coming of God's kingdom. Jesus teaches his disciples to pray saying "your kingdom come. . ." Jesus is God's perfect and ideal representative on earth, incomparably better than any other. He is not "nearly divine" as human beings (Ps. 8), but he is truly the "Son of God." He has power over creation; he stills storms because the winds obey him.

We see in Jesus' life an intensification of the battle between God's kingdom and that of the enemy, the adversary of God, and his helpers. It is the same battle we frequently meet in the Old Testament and which often troubles readers of the Bible.[30] This battle is visible in the story of the healing of a boy with an evil spirit in Luke 9:37–45. The evil spirit is very destructive for the boy and causes chaos.[31] Jesus heals the boy, and the people who witness the miracle are all "astonished at the majesty of God" (Luke 9:43, ESV). The work of Jesus Christ proclaims God's greatness and majesty.

One day everyone will recognize Jesus' rule over the earth, according to Philippians 2:9–11. Ephesians 6 and the book of Revelation discuss the battle between God and his adversaries. It is in Revelation that we often meet "universal" language like "from every tribe and language and people and nation" (Rev. 5:9) in the context of words which praise the Kingship of God. Revelation frequently uses language and vocabulary from the Old Testament.

At the end of the Bible, God creates new heavens and a new earth, linking the beginning in Genesis 1–2 with the fulfilment. Then God's Kingship will be visible everywhere and it will last forever. The throne of God and of the Lamb is at the heart of the new kingdom (Rev. 22:1–3).

The covenant

In addition to creation and God's Kingship, there is yet another central theological theme in the Old Testament that helps us to think about a framework for the ethical commands and laws – namely, the concept of covenant.

God consolidates his relationship with Israel by entering into a covenant with them. God also made covenants with Noah (Gen. 6:18; 9:9–17) and with Abram (Abraham) and his descendants (Gen. 15 and 17). Yet when we deal with the laws and commands in the Old Testament, it is the covenant with the people of Israel at Mount Sinai in particular which is essential. We find the details of this covenant in Exodus 19–24.

Covenant in the ancient Near East and in the Bible

There has been much discussion among scholars regarding the character and content of the biblical concept of covenant. Scholars have also studied the origins of the covenant. It is beyond the scope of the present book to deal with this discussion extensively; we will mention only a few important points. In general:

- The concept of covenant is very old and was well known in the world of which Israel was part. Covenants made thousands of years ago have been found in the Middle East.
- A covenant begins, consolidates, establishes or renews a relationship between partners. Covenants

could deal with all sorts of relationships, not only
political ones. Relationship, loyalty, and faithfulness
are key concepts in any covenant.
◆ A covenant connects two partners, who in most cases
   are not equals.

George E. Mendenhall first pointed out some of the
interesting similarities between the covenant at Sinai
and Hittite vassal treaties.[33] The Hittites lived in Asia
Minor (modern day Turkey), and their vassal treaties
date from the second millennium BC. Mendenhall studied treaties from the fifteenth to the twelfth centuries BC.
The treaties are agreements between a lord and his vassal – between a mighty king and a ruler of a minor state
who was his subordinate. Mendenhall discovered that
these covenants were formulated according to a fixed
pattern. The lord, who initiates the covenant, first intro-
duces himself in the "preamble." Then he reminds the
vassal of what he has done for him in the past. Next
come stipulations, which are the terms the vassal has to
obey, followed by instructions to write them down and
preserve the document. Witnesses are mentioned, and
finally blessings and curses are formulated – the consequences of which depend on whether or not the vassal
keeps the stipulations of the covenant.

There are several obvious similarities between these
treaties and parts of the Old Testament.

In the Ten Commandments in Exodus 20 we recognize the following elements:

◆ "I am the LORD your God" – introduction of the speaker
◆ "who brought you out of Egypt, out of the land of
   slavery" – historical prologue, which mentions what
   the LORD has done for his people (the "lord" for his
   "vassal")

- Only after these elements do we find the commandments, the "stipulations" that the "vassal," Israel,
  should keep
- The people themselves are the witnesses (v. 18)
- The whole covenant was written down, but that is
  only mentioned in chapter 24.

Thus we recognize a number of elements from the
Hittite vassal treaties, although they do not occur in any
strict order.

The structure of the book of Deuteronomy shares
even more elements in common with the Hittite vassal
treaties:

- Introduction of the speaker (and the hearers) (1:1–5)
- Historical prologue (1:6 – 4:49)
- General stipulations (5 – 11)
- Detailed stipulations (12 – 26)
- Blessings and curses (27 – 28)
- Witnesses (30:19; 31:19; 32)
- Instructions about the storage and public reading of
  the document (31:9–13, 24–26)[34]

One important similarity between the extrabiblical texts
and the Torah is the way that both introduce the
speaker, the initiator of the covenant. The documents
begin by enumerating exactly what the speaker has
already done for the vassal. The Ten Commandments
begin by reminding us of the special relationship God
has with his people. God saved them from the terrible
slavery in Egypt. The laws and commandments that follow – "rules for life," or guidelines for how to live as the
covenant people – are based on this secure relationship
of trust that God has established with them. God did not
subordinate his people by force; he does not establish a

covenant with them based on his victory over them, as is the case in vassal treaties. It is rather through his love and grace, and because he has kept his promises to the patriarchs, that God enters into this specific relationship with Israel and consolidates it in the covenant at Sinai. Neither is Israel expected to "repay" God. The commandments and laws are about living as a people who have already been saved from slavery in Egypt. As Wenham says,

> Israel is enjoined to love the LORD with all her heart, soul and strength. To walk after, cleave to, and to love him. Though it has been correctly pointed out that these are the actions required of loyal treaty partners, and that love and fear of God is expressed chiefly through keeping his commandments, it is wrong to reduce love to obedience. It is obedience, but more than obedience . . . The ethico-religious goal . . . involved both loyalty to God and an enjoyment of his presence.[35]

Moshe Weinfeld distinguishes two types of ancient contracts, and this distinction is also illuminating for the biblical concept of covenant: there are "covenants of grant" and "treaties."[36] In "covenants of grant" it is a sovereign who takes obligations upon himself concerning his vassal, rather than the other way around. A mighty king would make a treaty with a minor ruler out of gratitude, in order to reward the minor ruler for his loyalty towards him. This is the kind of covenant that God makes with Abraham and David – consolidating existing relationships in covenants that contain God's promises to them (see Gen. 17 and 2 Sam. 7).

The covenant with Israel, on the other hand, is a "treaty" type of covenant because it contains stipulations that the people should keep. As we have seen, the

Hittite vassal treaties contained important stipulations that the covenant partner should keep. The stipulations form the core of these treaties, and it is the responsibility of the subordinate ruler to keep these "commandments." We can compare the laws and commands in Exodus and Deuteronomy with such stipulations.

In the ancient Near East, an essential component of treaties and covenants was loyalty to the stronger partner, the initiator of the contract. Loyalty is also the issue in the first three commandments of the Decalogue, or the Ten Commandments.

Differences

There clearly are striking similarities between the Hittite vassal treaties and the book of Deuteronomy. Yet the latter is a different kind of document from a political vassal treaty. Deuteronomy is a theological text – a text that wants to make explicit the relationship between God and his people Israel. This relationship is different from that between a lord and his subordinate vassal. Deuteronomy 7:7–8 clearly states that God chose the people of Israel out of love, in his mercy and grace. These verses also continue the themes and action of Genesis and Exodus: in his covenant with Israel God is reaffirming the promises he made to the patriarchs,[37] just as he did when he called Moses (see Exod. 3:6, 15, 16).

Another difference between the secular covenants and the covenant between God and Israel (or David or Abraham) becomes clear when we study other treaties from the ancient Near East. In 1985, Mendenhall published his research on a covenant text from Byblos (in modern-day Lebanon). This text deals primarily with loyalty to the sovereign and prohibits every possible form of disloyalty in words, thoughts or actions.[38] The biblical text also requires Israel to be loyal to God ("You shall have no other gods before me"), but God does not establish this condition out of anxiety, as if he were afraid that his reign would be ended by rebellion. And even when God's people are breaking the covenant – as we read, for example, in Jeremiah 11 – God in his great mercy promises to make a new covenant (Jer. 31:31–34).

Covenant of grace

It is clear from Deuteronomy 7:7–8 that love is the foundation of Israel's election. It is by God's grace that he chose Israel. The first chapters of Deuteronomy remind the people of all the wonderful things God has done for them. As we have seen, the specific stipulations and regulations that follow in chapters 12–26 flow out of this relationship. God's people are to behave in a "godly" way as an appropriate response to God's redeeming acts. It is therefore clear that Israel does not "become" the people of God by keeping his commandments. They already are God's people – and that is why they are expected to live like that. They have not been saved by "works," but by "grace."

Laws in the ancient Near East and in the Bible

In addition to studying the forms of covenants and treaties in the ancient Near East, it is also worth looking at ancient law books from Old Testament times. Such comparison is helpful because it enables us to see how biblical law is unique as well as how it is similar to the laws of Israel's contemporaries – for example, in the language used.

Laws are usually not concerned with two parties who are in a covenantal relationship, but rather with establishing rules within a particular land. Often the king was the one who unilaterally decreed laws for his people. As Shalom M. Paul notes, however, in Israel the laws were an integral part of the covenant, essential for their existence as the covenant people:

> Treaties and legal collections are common throughout the Ancient Near East, but only in Israel does a legal collection embody the basis for the covenantal agreement between a deity and his elect. Only in Israel is there an inextricable relationship between covenant and law. The future of this nation now becomes predicated upon the observance of covenantal law.[39]

Discoveries in the ancient Near East have revealed that law books had existed for a long period in the world of ancient Israel. One of the best known examples is the law book of the Babylonian king Hammurabi, which can probably be dated around 1700 BC.[40] King Hammurabi made his own laws and wanted to show that he was a just and good king.[41] The gods allegedly gave him wisdom and knowledge to make laws, and he presented them to the gods hoping to receive their approval. Thus the author of the law book of Hammurabi was the king himself, although he attributes the laws to the guidance of the gods. In other countries, such as Assyria, the king was also the lawgiver. The Old Testament, however, emphasizes the fact that God himself is the author of the laws – and not Moses or an earthly king. Moses simply received them; he is not a royal, but a prophetic, figure. In the words of J. Gordon McConville:

> If the rule of gods in Assyria was expressed by means of a king who dominated every sphere of the nation's life,

Yahweh in contrast was the one who gave land, upheld justice and conducted wars.[42]

In Mesopotamia, the region Hammurabi came from, every new king would make his own laws.[43] He could build on earlier laws, but there was no normative binding law for all times. In contrast, the laws of Moses – or rather, the laws Moses received – are meant to be the only binding rules for Israel now and in the future. Ze'ev Falk notes:

> The right of lawmaking was not mentioned among the royal privileges; on the contrary, the king was 'to keep all the words of this law and these statutes' (Deuteronomy 17:19). . . . The law was not the creation of kingship but its basis and prerequisite.[44]

The fact that kingship and legislation were not connected in the Old Testament also meant that the king had to submit himself to the laws God had given. His actions were evaluated in their light and could be critically assessed. As Leon Epsztein remarks:

> . . . in Israel the king is not god as the Pharaoh is, nor his vicar, as the Babylonian prince is. The submission of the king to the will of Yahweh was constantly required; as the instrument and servant of God he has to act in accord with the divine will.[45]

In Mesopotamia, the government and the king had to preserve the order in the cosmos and society. Order was essential in the life of the individual and contrasted with the chaos out of which he had been born. In Israel, however, every individual was personally responsible when it came to keeping the law and commands. Maintaining order by keeping the law was not just the task of king or government. The people of Israel themselves were subject to God's law and, in the case of disobedience, they were summoned by the prophets.

Because the laws of the Torah were not only authoritative for the time of Moses, the Old Testament frequently refers back to them – for example in Hosea 4:2 and Jeremiah 7:9, which clearly echo the Ten Commandments.

The laws of Hammurabi are secular, not religious. They are laws about everyday life but not about religious observances. In the Old Testament, however, not only are there many laws about the worship of God, but all legislation is connected with Israel's relationship to God – even that which deals with apparently mundane matters. The reason for this is that, for God's people, there were no divisions between "secular" and "religious" areas of life. We will explore this concept in more detail below. Every sin in Israel is a sin against God.

The knowledge and observance of laws in the Old Testament is not only the king's business, but that of the whole nation. Even the children were taught to observe them. Laws in the Old Testament are relevant for each individual and for the people as a whole. To quote Epsztein again:

> The second-person singular address which Yahweh uses to the faithful in the codes of the Pentateuch indicates that he is addressing the whole people, everyone. By the will of God the whole society becomes the repository of the law and is responsible for it and its application. Every individual who is part of the community is involved. The laws dictated by God are not just communicated vertically (from God to the faithful) but are also propagated horizontally, in a democratic way, from man to man.[46]

Holiness

The Old Testament laws are more than just strict rules, more than simple do's and don'ts. The Torah is a way of life for the people of God, who are meant to be a model, a paradigm for the world. What does that model look like?

In Israel God created a special place on earth where the rules of life could be seen – which, as we saw above in the discussion of creation, were originally intended for the whole world. They are the rules of the kingdom of God. Israel was meant to keep these rules as they lived as the people of God. In studying the laws of the Torah we can see what God's ideal society looks like. The whole of life is meant to be a celebration of God's glory and should be wholly dedicated to him. In every aspect of life people could see that Israel was the people of God: in their food, their clothing, their rhythm of work and rest, their treatment of animals.

A core text here is Leviticus 19:1, "Be holy because I, the LORD your God, am holy." Holiness is not just perfection, or being without sin, as God is. It also means "set apart." When people in the Bible are called "holy," it means that they are set apart for God and dedicated to him alone. This was specifically the case with the priests in Israel, as Exodus 29:1 says: "This is what you are to do to consecrate them, so they may serve me as priests. . ." While the priests have a separate position in Israel, the ordinary Israelites are also called to be holy in all they do.

An idea related to holiness is that of wholeness, which means that God's people, saved from Egypt, should live whole lives as a sacrifice to God. As a nation they were set apart and chosen to serve him with full dedication.[47] That is what all of these prescriptions in the Torah, which sometimes seem painstaking to us, are about:

Israel was different and should live in a different way from the surrounding nations because God is different. He is the Holy One. The people of Israel were to dedicate themselves to serving God exclusively, excluding other gods who played such an important part in the lives of other nations. In practice, the danger was not that Israel would forget God completely, but that they would think that they could combine worshiping him with what the Canaanite religion had to offer. The first commandment, "no other gods," continued to be very relevant.

Yet King Jeroboam set up two golden calves in sanctuaries, which he thought would be acceptable to the Israelites: "Here are your gods, O Israel, who brought you up out of Egypt" (1 Kgs. 12:28). Jeroboam argued that the Israelites could pretend the calves were just "innocent symbols" of God, but the Torah makes it very clear that this was an impossible combination. Bulls were also important in the Canaanite religion, as part of their fertility cult. Images of God were expressly forbidden: the living God is unique and he is invisible, incomparable to anything visible or man-made. The people should in no way identify or even compare him with a visible object.

The story of the golden calf in Exodus 32 stems from the same problem: the people wanted a visible representation so that they could see their God. But the calf was a poor representation of the God who brought them out of Egypt.

The requirement of total dedication to God alone, just as God himself is One and a God of wholeness, finds eloquent expression in the last book of the Torah as well:

> Hear, O Israel: The LORD our God, the LORD is one. Love the LORD your God with all your heart and with all your soul and with all your strength. (Deut. 6:4–5)

When we read on in Deuteronomy 6 it becomes clear that these words should influence each member of God's people every day, in all we do and say:

> These commandments that I give you today are to be upon your hearts. Impress them on your children. Talk about them when you sit at home and when you walk along the road, when you lie down and when you get up. Tie them as symbols on your hands and bind them on your foreheads. Write them on the doorframes of your houses and on your gates. (Deut. 6:6–9)

To this day, pious Jews repeat these words every day.

Both obedience and disobedience were not without consequences, as is clear from Deuteronomy 27 and 28. These chapters contain curses and blessings that are not unlike those we find in many vassal treaties from other nations.[48] Both the curses and the blessings became realities in the sequel to Israel's history. They are the connecting thread through the Old Testament. The prophets in particular built their message upon the covenant and the fact that Israel was often in danger of bringing the curses upon itself through disobedience.

Prophetic criticism

The Old Testament prophets constantly reminded the people of their responsibility to keep the requirements of the covenant into which their forefathers had entered. They constantly reminded the people of Israel, and in particular the responsible leaders (such as the kings and the priests), that they had been chosen by God to live according to his call.

In the Jewish arrangement of the books of what Christians call the Old Testament, the books of Samuel and Kings belong to the "prophetic" books, and not to the historical books. These books are indeed prophetic descriptions of history, since they evaluate the kings of Israel and Judah from the point of view of what they did with the law of God. Throughout Israel's history there were prophets who warned kings and the people when they were in danger of ignoring the Torah.

The prophet Nathan rebuked King David after he had committed adultery with Bathsheba and had her husband murdered to hide his sin (2 Sam. 11–12). The prophet Elijah rebuked King Ahab after he had taken the vineyard of Naboth – which in itself was against the regulations in the Torah – and also murdered this man (1 Kgs. 21). Naboth knew the law: the land was to remain in the family. That was one of the main rules in the Torah: every Israelite family had the right to a piece of land.[49] A king in Israel was never above the law – he had to obey it just like everybody else. Ahab's wife Jezebel, however, came from the foreign region of Tyre and Sidon, where the king could do whatever he wanted. She could not imagine that her husband Ahab could not achieve whatever he wanted.

In the same vein, the so-called Writing Prophets reminded the people again and again of the laws and commands of God. Sometimes they quote laws nearly word-for-word, and such passages give us insight in the essence of Israelite ethics. Jeremiah, for instance, preached to the people at the gate of the temple:

If you really change your ways and your actions and deal with each other justly, if you do not oppress the alien, the fatherless or the widow and do not shed innocent blood in this place, and if you do not follow other gods to your

own harm, then I will let you live in this place, in the land
I gave to your forefathers for ever and ever. . . . Will you
steal and murder, commit adultery and perjury, burn
incense to Baal and follow other gods you have not
known . . .? (Jer. 7:5–7, 9)

This passage contains specific commands about care for the
weak people in society – "the alien, the fatherless or the
widow," those without normal social security. These words
contain a sort of summary of the Ten Commandments as
well: there should be no stealing, murder, adultery, perjury
or idolatry. Jeremiah relates the question of whether the
people will be allowed to stay in the promised land or not
to their keeping of the commandments, in the same way as
Deuteronomy relates these things in 28:64–68. Removal
from the land was among the sanctions in the covenant
treaty God made with his people.

   From a certain moment in Israel's history onwards,
the prophets could not but pronounce judgement on the
sins of the people, because for a long time they had
refused to repent. The prophets had to announce that
God would make a (temporary) end to their living in the
promised land, because God's people had not kept the
covenant stipulations, the commandments of God.
Jeremiah says:

Why has the land been ruined and laid waste like a desert
that no one can cross? The LORD said, "It is because they
have forsaken my law, which I set before them; they have
not obeyed me or followed my law. Instead, they have followed the stubbornness of their hearts; they have followed
the Baals, as their fathers taught them." Therefore [as a
consequence], ". . . I will scatter them among nations that
neither they nor their fathers have known . . ." (Jer.
9:12b–15a, 16)

Summary and conclusions

The establishment of the covenant between God and Israel is a pivotal point in the Old Testament, but God's history with humankind began long before the events at Sinai. As the Creator of heaven and earth, God wants to be recognized as the only King among all the nations. Yet he chose one nation and established a special relationship with that people in order that they might be a "model" for the other nations in a world defiled by sin. God established that relationship with this people through an agreement called a covenant.

People in the ancient Near East were well acquainted with the concepts of covenants and law books. The covenant between God and Israel, however, has its own unique characteristics. The differences are mainly derived from the fact that the Sinai covenant is not an agreement between human beings but between God, the Creator and the Savior of his people, and Israel. The covenant and the commands belonging to it are theocentric: God is the starting point and the orientation point for Israel and its laws.

The covenant between God and Israel is primarily based on what God has done for his people – saving them from their enemies in Egypt. This act of salvation, however, is deeply rooted in history – in the promises God previously made to Abraham, Isaac, and Jacob. It is only by grace that Israel exists as the people of God. God chose Abraham, Isaac, Jacob, and their descendants, Israel, because in his grace he wanted to do so.

The covenant includes stipulations that the Israelites need to keep in order to live as the people of God. Blessings or curses will result from Israel's obedience or disobedience – the most visible of those blessings being their possession of the promised land. Israel does not

become the people of God by keeping his commandments, but they will show themselves outwardly to be
his people by keeping his commandments.

On one hand, the covenant with Israel is exclusive:
God has set this particular people apart from the other
nations. On the other hand it is not exclusive, because
God will not neglect the other nations. God intended the
blessing of Israel to extend to others. The blessings as
well as the laws that God gave to Israel should give
other nations insight into the wisdom of the God of
Israel. As Moses said,

> Observe them [the decrees and laws of v. 5] carefully, for
> this will show your wisdom and understanding to the
> nations, who will hear about all these decrees and say,
> "Surely this great nation is a wise and understanding
> people." What other nation is so great as to have their gods
> near them the way the LORD our God is near us whenever
> we pray to him? And what other nation is so great as to
> have such righteous decrees and laws as this body of laws
> I am setting before you today? (Deut. 4:6–8)

Questions for further reflection

1. What would you consider to be the core of the Old
   Testament, and why?
2. What are some of the implications of the belief that
   humans are made in the image of God?
3. Based on our exploration of the source and purpose of
   the law, why do you think the Jewish people celebrate
   the law (in an annual festival called *Simchat Torah*, or
   "the Joy of the Torah")?
4. What difference does it make in your life that God is
   the King of the earth?

Proposals for a Framework

In Chapter 2 we looked at the Old Testament as a whole from the point of view of its first part, the Torah. In order to gain a better understanding of their essence and meaning, is it now possible to arrange the Old Testament laws and decrees in a theological framework? The first five books of the Old Testament, in particular, contain such a large number of rules, decrees, and laws that such a framework would be most helpful. All of these prescriptions about slavery, animals, the land, sacrifices, witchcraft, sexual conduct, leprosy, and so on are quite bewildering.

We are not the first to make this attempt, and in this chapter we borrow valuable insights from others as we study some of the frameworks that have been proposed.

The Ten Commandments as the core?

The commandments that God gave to Israel play a crucial role in the context of the covenant between God and Israel. They are an integral part of it, as we saw in Chapter 2. These laws are not conditions for being the people of God. God has chosen his people solely by his grace and election. The commandments are, however, the rules for *living* as the people of God, and obeying them is a condition for receiving the blessings reserved for God's people in the promised land.

Many theologians have very little idea about what to do with the numerous and diverse laws found in the Old Testament. Often they will deal with the Decalogue in some detail and virtually ignore the other commandments. Some consider the Decalogue, a brief text found in Exodus 20 and Deuteronomy 5, to be the core of Old Testament ethics. Sometimes this seems to be the most convenient way of dealing with the problem. It is little wonder that the church has taken, and continues to take, the same attitude.

Convenience is certainly not the motive behind the extensive work that Walter Kaiser has done on Old Testament ethics, but he is among those who take the Ten Commandments as the core.[50] Kaiser also deals with the main complexes of laws and decrees as Old Testament scholarship usually distinguishes them: the Book of the Covenant (Exod. 20:22 – 23:33), the Law of Holiness (Lev. 18 – 20) and Deuteronomy. Kaiser further sees "holiness" as an overarching theme for the laws in the Old Testament – that God wants Israel to reflect his holiness in all aspects of life.[51]

Kaiser is obviously convinced of the authority of the Bible. At the same time, however, he states that there is a difference in the degree of authority of the various laws and decrees:

> We conclude by emphasizing the organic perfection and truthfulness of God in each and every revelatory event and disclosure of his Word: yet, we also want to stress the fact that it was successive and truly in the context of history with all the humanness, primitiveness, error, and unevenness of growth that that fact implies. Only by carefully

regarding these twin truths will we be able to properly assess the element of progressive revelation in Old Testament morality.[52]

Kaiser concludes that the so-called ceremonial laws are no longer essential for Christians. On the other hand the "moral" law, in particular the Ten Commandments, remains valid. Kaiser refers to Jesus' words in Matthew 23:23 to indicate that Jesus himself makes a distinction between relevant and less relevant laws: "Woe to you, teachers of the law and Pharisees, you hypocrites! You give a tenth of your spices – mint, dill and cummin. But you have neglected the more important matters of the law – justice, mercy and faithfulness."[53]

Threefold division

Theologians often distinguish between different types of law in the same way as Kaiser does. Traditionally these theologians see a threefold division consisting of:

- moral laws, like the Ten Commandments;
- civil laws, which addressed issues in Israelite society;
- ceremonial laws, which set down regulations for the cult and other rituals, such as sacrifices.

Those who divide the Old Testament laws in this way usually state that the moral laws are still valid for the Christian church, but the other two types are not.

At first sight the distinction seems to be illuminating as we consider the contemporary relevance of Old Testament laws. Upon closer examination, however, we begin to see that it is less helpful than it first appears. A strong objection to this division is that neither the Old

nor the New Testament explicitly mentions these different categories of laws. In fact, there appears to be no
such distinction in the Old Testament.

Furthermore, such artificial divisions are not as clear-
cut as they might at first appear. For example, is the
commandment to keep the Sabbath a moral law? The
Old Testament itself gives several motives for keeping
the Sabbath. In the first place, God rested on the seventh
day and he blessed it (Exod. 20:11). We could therefore
see this commandment as a "moral" law. At the same
time it is a social law as well, given to ensure rest for
everybody – humans and animals. The explanation of
the commandment to keep the Sabbath in Deuteronomy
5:15 clearly refers to the hard times the people of Israel
endured in Egypt, and to the exodus. The Sabbath can
also be seen as a "civil" law, for its observance helps to
order society in a certain way. Leviticus 23:3 mentions
the Sabbath in the context of the festivals, and it can
therefore fall under the category of "ceremonial" law as
well.[54]

We conclude that, while the division between moral,
civil, and ceremonial laws may illuminate certain passages, it cannot serve as a hermeneutical principle for
the interpretation of the Torah as a whole.

In search of a framework

Different theologians have tried to categorize the Old
Testament laws in other ways in order to evaluate their
value for today's church. Yet nobody has found a division which is universally recognized and which deals
satisfactorily with all the complex issues involved. As
we have seen, the Old Testament itself does not establish
such a system either. There is no system to help us

distinguish between what is still valid and what is no longer valid. In fact, the whole Torah simply claims validity for all of Israel at all times. In so far as human beings have tried to design such a system, there is always the danger of leaving out essential elements and of reading the Old Testament in too narrow a way.

In his book *Toward Old Testament Ethics*, Kaiser tries to deal with nearly everything the Old Testament has to say in the area of ethics. He deals with a large number of rules and provides extensive biblical illustrations, thereby giving his book the character of a sort of "handbook" of Old Testament ethics. And yet, as we have seen, his overall framework is insufficient to handle all of the rules contained in the Old Testament.

We continue our search, therefore, for a theological framework that helps us to understand the Old Testament material on ethics as a whole. What do the laws say about God and about human beings? What do they teach us about contemporary problems? Such an overall framework may prevent us from using the Old Testament merely as a "book of rules" which we use in order to find "proof texts" for ethical problems, ancient and modern. With such a framework we will see that even if the Old Testament does not mention a certain issue, that does not mean it does not have anything to say about it. In addition we may find that, if we know their place in the Old Testament context, even issues which were typical for days gone by are still relevant for us.

Commands and narratives as paradigms

In his book *Old Testament Ethics: A Paradigmatic Approach*, Waldemar Janzen reacts to the fact that the Ten

Commandments are often considered to be the summit of Old Testament ethics. He interacts with different authors, such as Kaiser, who try to define the whole of Old Testament ethics from the Decalogue.[55] Janzen does agree that the Ten Commandments are essential in the Old Testament, since God gives them in the context of the Sinai covenant. In his opinion this does not mean, however, that the Decalogue deals with *all* ethical issues. He mentions other relevant passages, such as Leviticus 19:1–18 and Deuteronomy 27:15–26, which contain much of the same material as the Decalogue, but which also deal with other commands which are not irrelevant for us today.[56] Janzen's conclusion is that the Decalogue gives *examples* of ethical conduct without dealing with every aspect of life. The first two commandments are an exception to this.[57]

According to Janzen, the narrative parts of the Old Testament are at least as important as the laws and decrees. This insight is a valuable element in his work. Janzen is concerned that ethics should not be seen as a system of abstract, timeless principles that stand apart from the narratives in the Old Testament. He thinks Old Testament ethics is too often reduced to a fixed set of rules that are to be considered valid for all times and all nations. This is, he says, what often happens with the Ten Commandments. Janzen therefore clearly distances himself from Kaiser's method of systematizing the laws and commandments in reference to the Decalogue.[58] Whenever Old Testament ethics is reduced to a list of rules, Janzen remarks, the only question Christians have to ask is whether a certain rule is still valid for them or not. They no longer look at passages in their contexts.[59] Not a few authors reduce Old Testament ethics to an investigation of the laws in the Pentateuch, without considering the later parts of the Old Testament.[60]

Narratives

According to Janzen, not only do the Old Testament passages that contain laws and decrees have a *paradigmatic* function, but also the narrative material. The stories provide us with examples or case studies, both positive and negative. Reading or hearing the stories shapes the moral insight of the reader or hearer. Janzen distinguishes between several paradigmatic functions in the laws and stories: the familial, priestly, wisdom, royal, and prophetic paradigms. The familial paradigm is the most basic, from which the others have been derived.[61]

The familial paradigm is central in the Ten Commandments: the singular "thou" appeals to the father as the head of the clan. By addressing him God addresses the whole household. The father is required to keep the commandments together with the rest of the household. The presupposition is that he is able to influence their lives decisively. The commandment regarding the Sabbath sums up the various elements that constitute the whole household group (Exod. 20:10).[62]

Stories like the one about Abram and Lot in Genesis 13, the story of Ruth, and the sad story of Judges 19 all illustrate the familial paradigm. In these three stories we discover the importance of family relationships in a narrow sense (Abram and Lot), in a wider sense (the family of Elimelek in Ruth) and in an even wider sense still (the whole of Israel deals with what the tribe of Benjamin has done in Judges 19). According to Janzen, these stories deal with three important issues of the familial paradigm: life, land, and hospitality. This last issue comes clearly to the fore in the book of Ruth, and in Judges 19:23–24 in the person of the old man, who offers up his own daughter to protect his guest.[63]

Paradigm

This paradigmatic approach seems to provide a good perspective from which we can look at the whole of the Old Testament for its ethical relevance. In this respect, it is a better option than the detailed systematizing of Kaiser. As John Barton says, "'Torah' is a system by which to live the whole of life in the presence of God, rather than a set of detailed regulations to cover every individual situation in which a moral ruling might be called for."[64] The concept of paradigm seems to be of great importance in dealing with Old Testament ethics.

Chris Wright's definition of paradigm has certain advantages over Janzen's, however. Wright expounds this definition in *Living as the People of God*. "A paradigm is something used as a model or example for other cases where a basic principle remains unchanged, though details differ. . . . A paradigm is not so much imitated as applied. It is assumed that cases will differ but, when necessary adjustments have been made, they will conform to the observable pattern of the paradigm."[65]

We encounter an example of this type of paradigm, as Wright says, when we learn the grammar of a foreign language. In order to learn the regular (or irregular) verbs, students have to learn one example of each of them in its entire conjugation. The examples can then be applied to all regular (or irregular) verbs of the same type.

Applying Old Testament laws by reading them paradigmatically means that we look at the basic principles and try to adapt them to our modern times. In Leviticus 19:9, for instance, we read the command: "When you reap the harvest of your land, do not reap to the very edges of your field or gather the gleanings of your harvest." In our Western world, most people do not own land, and few poor people would reap the harvest on a farmer's land. However, the principle behind this commandment is that of sharing with the poor and caring for them – and this is as relevant today as it ever was.

Let us return to Wright's definition of paradigm. In his book *Walking in the Ways of the Lord*, Wright elaborates the concept of paradigm by giving two definitions used by the scientist and philosopher Thomas Kuhn.[66] On the one hand he describes a paradigm as all of the convictions, values, techniques that are shared by one particular group. On the other hand he uses the word paradigm to mean a concrete solution to a problem, which functions as an example for solving other problems of a similar kind.

Wright applies the two definitions to Israel in the Old Testament. The people of Israel share many convictions and values, which are essential to them, such as monotheism and belief in God as Creator. On the other hand, Israel itself is a paradigm, "a concrete model, a practical, culturally specific, experimental exemplar of the beliefs and values they embodied."[67] We can derive some basic principles from the way they dealt with certain issues. We could, for example, ask: How was the penal system organized in the Old Testament and what can we learn from it? Are there any rules in the Old Testament for dealing with other cultures? In answering this last question, we see that there are three possibilities: Israel was to absolutely reject some things; some things they tolerated but criticized; and some things they accepted. Our task then becomes one of scrutinizing these three possibilities within our framework to determine how we deal with equivalent contemporary issues.

Wright emphasizes that, in using the concept of paradigm, we are not assuming that human insights and development shaped Israel's rules and commands. God himself revealed them, and therefore they have authority. In the context of the culture of the ancient Near East, God formed a people for himself and shaped a community to which he revealed a new paradigm for understanding himself, the world, and humanity. God gave them laws to demonstrate that what he revealed was true. In Wright's own words:

> . . . within the parameters of ancient Near Eastern macroculture God brought into being a society through whom he both revealed a new paradigm of understanding God, the world and humanity, and actually modelled a framework of laws, institutions, conventions and customs, which experimentally demonstrated the truth of that revelation.[68]

Wright uses both of Kuhn's definitions here.

Janzen values Wright's study, but he chooses a different definition of paradigm than the grammatical illustration that Wright used in *Living as the People of God*.[69] With Wright's definition in mind, Janzen states:

> For our purposes, however, paradigm will be understood as a personally and holistically conceived image of a model (e.g., a wise person, good king) that imprints itself immediately and nonconceptually on the characters and actions of those who hold it.[67]

According to Janzen's approach, a paradigm is the sort of impression the reader gets when hearing the Old Testament stories. This impression, more or less consciously, influences the reader's concept of what is "wise," "good," and so on. Janzen uses the concept of paradigm in the context of stories. He hesitates to abstract general principles from biblical material –

especially from stories.[71] On the one hand, he exercises proper caution by being careful not to read stories only in order to derive principles or rules from them. In addition, single verses can only be understood by taking the larger context into consideration.

Janzen seems to have more objections to commands and principles, however, than Kaiser and Wright do. Both of the latter acknowledge the commands of the Old Testament as God's commands and principles. Janzen, on the other hand, argues that the text of the Old Testament has been formed by human beings over a long period, during which they developed their own thoughts. The text has only gradually become the canon of the Jews and Christians. Janzen's view becomes clear in what he writes about the Ten Commandments:

> A very different understanding of such laws emerges when one sees them, in light of our preceding considerations, as shorthand formulations of ethical values and imperatives emerging from a particular story – Israel's story – and as continuing to be defined by that story. Then they can no longer be seen as self-contained universal maxims, nor can they be loosened from the story in which they are embedded. . . . Whatever authority they hold over us is rooted in our acceptance of the story that defines them.[72]

Janzen sympathizes with Bruce Birch, who also writes about the paradigmatic function of the stories in the Old Testament. Birch argues that ethics was shaped by the centuries.[73] His approach is clear from the study that he wrote with Larry Rasmussen. They emphasize that we should not regard the Bible as the sole authority for moral conduct, as that is also shaped by the community of the church as it reads and discusses biblical texts and interprets them by its own authority. According to Birch and Rasmussen, we should not try to derive authoritative principles from the Bible.[74]

In his *Glimpses of a Strange Land*, Cyril Rodd declares that it is impossible to find a "whole thrust" of Old Testament ethics: there are too many inconsistencies in the Old Testament.[75] The only things we can do is to try to find "glimpses" of a "land" – a whole world of thinking and acting which is not our own. It is a "strange land." Efforts to find a unifying theme in the Bible are in vain. Rodd is opposed to a canonical or a synchronic reading of the Old Testament, which according to him must be studied in a historical-critical way in order to do justice to the variety of historical and theological contexts of its different parts. In Rodd's opinion one does not come to an ethical decision by looking at "what the Bible says," because we are all influenced by our own culture and presuppositions. There is no objectivity in the search for Old Testament ethics.[76] Besides, our problems are not the problems of the Old Testament. Even with regard to issues about which we might want to draw conclusions, the Old Testament actually means to say something different. When it gives instructions about caring for the poor, for example, Rodd maintains that this is more about individual charity than about a "just society."[77]

Rodd is, of course, absolutely correct in arguing that we are all influenced by our own world and culture. Behind his thinking, however, lies the idea that the Bible cannot tell us what to do. In Rodd's opinion, the Scriptures do not have the authority that evangelical Christians ascribe to them. As he says, ". . . the first requirement is to abandon the propositional view of revelation, and with it the belief in the Bible as an external authority."[78]

Rodd leaves the reader with very little information about how ethical thinking may have developed in Old

Testament times. Apart from his warnings that we
should not read more into the text than is actually given,
his major presupposition amounts to an abandonment
of the concept of the authority of Scripture – which
leaves us without any foundation for our thinking and
belief.

Revelation and paradigm

In any approach to Old Testament ethics it is important to
maintain the authority of the Bible as a basic principle,
essential for our reading of it. In the Torah, the people of
Israel are reminded time and again to keep the laws and
commands because God has given them. They are not the
invention of a king or even of Moses as a prophet. These
laws and commands claim to have authority, and we cannot just put that claim aside. The Ten Commandments, for
instance, are given to the people in the context of great
reverence, in which God first makes himself known to
Moses. So the evangelical Christian shares the faith of the
people of God who first received these laws.

Having accepted this authority, we need to understand what the different laws meant in their original
context. What is the principle behind the Old Testament
laws dealing with land? How do we apply that principle
in a world where many people do not own land to gen-
erate their income, as is the case in cities? The laws can
thus be used as "paradigms," as "models" or "examples." At the same time, as we have seen, Israel itself was
meant to be a paradigm in its existence and in its
his-tory. In the final chapter we will see that the ideals
for Israel can be ideals for the church as well.

In Israel we see how God's laws and regulations have
to do with the whole of life. Israel is meant to show

God's ideals for humanity and the world in the way it exists, lives, and acts. Even when Israel fails to do so, the prophets point out what they should be and do. They refer Israel back to its ideal, that is to say: to God's ideal.

The concept of a paradigm seems to be worth looking at in more detail. The paradigm, which is shown to us not only in the commands and laws, but also in the biblical stories and in the very existence of Israel, is that of a life lived as God wants us to live. That is more than merely "not stealing, not murdering, not lying." As Wenham puts it, ". . . ethics is much more than keeping the law."[79] The Old Testament is not just a handbook full of rules. Rather, God shows us the principles that are important to him through the commands he has given. It is in understanding these principles and obeying these commands that we live our lives as God intended.

Wright's design for Old Testament ethics

Let us take a closer look at Wright's concept of paradigm and the way he offers a framework for Old Testament ethics. In his *Living as the People of God* and *Walking in the Ways of the Lord* Wright uses three major topics, visualized in the shape of a triangle, as a key to understanding Old Testament ethics.[80]

"God" is first in the triangle. He takes the initiative in calling Israel to be his people. It is through his grace that they are redeemed. Their thankful answer is to follow his commandments. Salvation precedes the commandments: "I am the LORD your God, who brought you out of Egypt, out of the land of slavery" (Exod. 20:2). Old Testament ethics is also "God-centred"[81] in its content and its motivation. Wright says, "Personal experience of God is turned into motivation for consistent ethical behaviour."[82] Because of what God has done for them, Israel should do the same for others, as in the case of treating slaves in a humane way. Ethics is about reflecting God's holy character: "Be holy because I, the LORD your God, am holy" (Lev. 19:2). Furthermore, Wright says, the fact that God delivered his people from slavery is an incentive for treating slaves and other weak people in society in a humane way (Exod. 23:9).

"The people" form the second corner of the triangle. They are meant to be God's "paradigm" in the world. They "model" how God originally intended human beings to behave and to live with him and with one another. They are a "prototype" of God's ideal and show a "pattern" for how God meant the world to be. The priests in Israel were a model for the people, but Israel itself is "priestly" as well: "Although the whole earth is mine, you will be for me a kingdom of priests and a holy nation" (Exod. 19:5–6). Christians can learn from the Old Testament what God's principles are by looking at the way he deals with his people. The concept of "paradigm" does not mean that Christians simply need to "copy" Israel's laws, but rather that they learn from these laws what God intended to say through them.

"The land" is the third corner in Wright's triangle. The promise of the land and its fulfillment play a major part in the Pentateuch. The land is God's gift to his people, their inheritance. There are responsibilities, however, that accompany this gift. Each family of God's chosen people has the right to own a part of the promised land. This means that rich people cannot use their power to claim other people's land, as the story of Naboth and King Ahab eloquently illustrates (1 Kgs. 21).

Wright expands this basic triangle by placing it in the wider context of the whole world and its future. Israel has a paradigmatic function in a fallen world, and the way they live in the promised land is paradigmatic in a fallen creation.[83] Furthermore, there is an eschatological element, because Israel's way of living in the promised land foreshadows how one day God will redeem humankind and be their God, and also how the earth will be a new creation.[84] We will look at the place of the Christian church in this triangle in the final chapter of this book.

Several scholars have critiqued Wright's concept, among them Eckart Otto, who argues that Wright pays insufficient attention to the historical distance between the Bible and modern times. According to Otto there is a big gap between the Bible and today; Old Testament ethics can therefore only be descriptive, not prescriptive. Otto asserts that Wright seems to ignore the complex character of Old Testament laws in their historical development as well as the complex character of modern times.[85]

Otto's critique, however, is based on an altogether different way of reading the Bible. Wright would not deny the complexity of Bible passages, as is clear from his other works as well, but in principle he affirms the authority and relevance of the Bible for today. As we have seen, to draw out principles for modern times is not an easy job, but Wright does well to adapt the relevant data of Old Testament ethics to modern economics and politics in a way which is at least worth considering.[86]

Each framework has its disadvantages. Frameworks are always a simplification of a more complex reality. Still, Wright has made a valuable contribution to an understanding of Old Testament ethics without losing sight of the context of the whole canon of the Christian church.

Basic keys to Old Testament ethics

From all that we have looked at thus far we can define some basic principles of Old Testament ethics:

1. From the beginning, from the moment of creation, ethics is part of the history of humankind (see Chapter 2). From the beginning God has given guidelines for living in his presence. God has created each person, and humans are God's royal representatives. Old Testament ethics does not start with the Ten Commandments.
2. Old Testament ethics is based on God's grace. God saved Israel from Egypt and he chose them as his people. By living as God intends them to, Israel responds to God's grace with thankfulness. Israel does not *become* God's people by obeying his commandments, but in doing just that they show the reality of what it means to be the people of God.
3. In the covenant on Sinai God establishes a special relationship with Israel, with the intention that he will ultimately extend this relationship to include the whole world. God incorporates his perfect plans and purposes in Israel's laws and commands. Israel is meant to present a model, a paradigm for the whole world, in order that other nations may come to know and serve the God of Israel.
4. Old Testament ethics is "theocratic," or rather "theocentric." God gives the laws, and therefore they are good. They are life-giving because God is the Giver of life.
5. Furthermore, there is no neat division between a "spiritual" and a "physical" life, between "horizontalism" and "verticalism." We are to live our lives in the light of God's presence. Old Testament ethics is thus a *way of living*.

To this list we may add a few more important issues that we have not yet covered in detail.

6. The land plays an important role in Israel's history. The possession of the promised land is, so to speak, the "thermometer" of Israel's faith. This is the case not only in the Pentateuch, but also throughout the Old Testament. The prophets deal with this issue quite extensively.

A good example is Hosea 4:1–3:

> Hear the word of the LORD, you Israelites, because the LORD has a charge to bring against you who live in the land:
> "There is no faithfulness, no love, no acknowledgement of God in the land.
> There is only cursing, lying and murder, stealing and adultery;
> they break all bounds, and bloodshed follows bloodshed.
> Because of this the land mourns, and all who live in it waste away;
> the beasts of the field and the birds of the air and the fish of the sea are dying."

A case is made against the people of Israel because of their lack of faithfulness, love, and acknowledgement of God. The people are not living with God in such a way that it is visible in daily life. Verse 2 refers to the Ten Commandments: "cursing, lying and murder, stealing and adultery." Relationships have been obstructed, both horizontally and vertically. Verse 3 mentions the consequences of sinning against God and fellow members of the covenant people. The land and the animals are mourning and dying, the land and the whole of creation are suffering because of the sins against God and others.

The ruin and death described in verse 3 contrast with the story of creation in Genesis 1. Sin causes the destruction of the beauty of creation. It causes death and brings back the initial chaos that existed before God formed heaven and earth.

Jeremiah refers to creation in the same way:

> I looked at the earth, and it was formless and empty;
> and at the heavens, and their light was gone.
> I looked at the mountains, and they were quaking; all the hills were swaying.
> I looked, and there were no people; every bird in the sky had flown away.
> I looked, and the fruitful land was a desert; all its towns lay in ruins before the LORD, before his fierce anger. (4:23–26)

Sin defiles the land: "I brought you into a fertile land to eat its fruit and rich produce. But you came and defiled my land and made my inheritance detestable" (Jer. 2:7).

7. Ethics in the Old Testament is not (only) about individuals, but also about community. In the Western world we have become more and more individualistic so that ethics has often become a matter of "what I like or do not like not to do." It is about individual decisions that, it is claimed, only concern ourselves. In the Old Testament, by contrast, ethics is based in community and concerns the whole of society. My personal actions and choices do have consequences for the whole of God's people of which I am part.[87] This does not mean, of course, that the Old Testament is not interested in individuals as such. God is said to be concerned about individuals like Abraham, Isaac,

and Jacob, and the poet of Psalm 23 can write: "The
LORD is *my* shepherd . . ." There is a balance between
the individual and the corporate. Many psalms seem
to have had a function in the life of Israel's community, too. In the same way, God made promises to
Abraham personally yet extended them to all the
nations on earth, as we have seen.

Individuals and community are interrelated. This connection is particularly visible in the person of the king. A
good king is a blessing to the land (Ps. 72:12–17), but a
godless king is destructive to land and people, as the
books of Kings and Chronicles illustrate.

Individual Israelites saw themselves as part of their
people's history, as we can see in Deuteronomy 26:1–11.
This passage gives instructions for offering the firstfruits
in the promised land. The individual Israelites stand
before the priest and speak words in which they identify themselves with the history of Israel. They use
words like "my" and "us" as if they had personally been
present at the exodus from Egypt: "My father was a
wandering Aramean, and he went down into Egypt . . .
But the Egyptians ill-treated us . . ." Jews still celebrate
the exodus today by speaking about how *we* were slaves
in Egypt.

H. Wheeler Robinson introduced the term "corporate
personality" for this way of speaking. "Corporate solidarity" seems to be a better phrase for what he meant,
because the individual personality was still valued in
Israel. The relationship between the individual and community in Israel was determined by solidarity on the
basis of the covenant.[88]

To all of this we may add that several Hebrew words
which are relevant in Old Testament ethics have a meaning which transcends the individual. Important words

like *chesed*, or "loyalty," "love," "faithfulness" and *tsedaqa*, or "justice," should be seen in a covenantal context. As Vriezen argues:

> Men are closely linked together . . . as Yahweh lives in a Covenant-relation with man, man is also linked with his fellow-man by *chesed* (faithfulness). Men linked together by Yahweh are brothers, Israel is a community of brothers. . . . The background of the words "faithfulness," "righteousness" and "justice," without which the Israelite community cannot exist, is the idea of the Covenant.[89]

Thus the Old Testament concept of community does not just pertain to the family, to people who are related because they belong to certain tribes, but it is also based on religion. The Old Testament is not just about "God and my soul' (and neither is the New), but about living as part of God's family in the context of the covenant relationship.

Individualistic ethics do not occur in the Old Testament. That does not mean, however, that individuals are not held responsible for their own deeds. Note, for example, the fact that the Ten Commandments are in the singular although their context is the covenant with the people as a whole. The words of Walther Zimmerli are worth quoting at some length:

> The constantly recurring debate over whether the Decalogue is addressed to the individual or to the people as a whole can only make it clear how self-evidently the appeal to the individual is here set in an appeal to all Israel. The analogous observation can be made in the discussion of the "I" in the Psalms, where it is fundamentally impossible to maintain the distinction between the individual "I" and the community of the people of God. Similarly, there is

no individual morality to be distinguished from responsibility in and for the community.[91]

In Ezekiel 18 the prophet explains that people had not been taken into exile because of what previous generations had done wrong, but because of their own deeds. Neither can they hide behind the good deeds of their parents (vv. 10–13). Ezekiel 18 also gives us a good insight into what was seen as the ideal and the just. The issues mentioned remind us of the Ten Commandments: no idolatry, care for the oppressed and the poor, honesty in dealing with money, and so on. In the past, scholars believed that this chapter shows that there had been a move from communal thinking to more individualistic thinking in Israel, but it is clear that the community and the individual can never be pitted against each other anywhere in the Old Testament. As Elmer Martens says, "Individuals are important, but individualism is not."[92]

In the final chapter we will return to the issue of the New Testament and the individual in the context of ethics.

Questions for further reflection

1. What role do the Ten Commandments play in your life? And what role do they play in your church, if you attend one?
2. Do you think we should adopt the Ten Commandments as a guideline in society or in politics?
3. How do you normally make ethical decisions? Are you influenced by the church, your family, friends, the Bible? How important are others in decision making?
4. In what way is the life of Jesus a paradigm?

4

Food Laws: Applying the Framework

We have explored some basic principles in the Old Testament that can be used to construct a framework for Old Testament ethics. This chapter, together with the following two chapters, present three examples of Old Testament law to which we will apply the framework that consists of the idea of paradigm and the seven basic principles from Chapter 3, above. These three cases will serve to illustrate the observations we have made thus far. We will look in this chapter at the laws regarding clean and unclean food in Leviticus 11. In Chapter 5 we will explore the laws from Deuteronomy 15 about debt cancellation in the Sabbath year. Then, in Chapter 6, we will apply this framework to the law concerning warfare in Deuteronomy 20. For people today in particular, the laws on food and warfare are difficult to understand – let alone to apply. These laws may even appear to corroborate the idea that the Old Testament is very different from the New Testament – and maybe even obsolete. It is worth looking carefully at these texts, however, in order to discover what they really are about and to see whether we can learn from them. Although it is difficult not to read them with prejudice, it is well worth the effort. In the final chapter, we will apply all of these principles to the church today.

The book of Leviticus contains all sorts of regulations and laws. There are regulations about different sacrifices (Lev. 1 – 7), instructions on priesthood (8 – 10), regulations about cleanness and uncleanness (11 – 15), laws concerning special days and feasts (16 and 23) and on special years (25). Leviticus 19 is the heart of the book. This chapter, which we will return to below, presents some very important laws in the framework of "holiness."

Leviticus 11 presents laws concerning clean and unclean animals. The following verses (vv. 1–12 and 44–47) give us a picture of what the chapter is about.[93]

The LORD said to Moses and Aaron, "Say to the Israelites: 'Of all the animals that live on land, these are the ones you may eat: You may eat any animal that has a split hoof completely divided and that chews the cud.

"'There are some that only chew the cud or only have a split hoof, but you must not eat them. The camel, though it chews the cud, does not have a split hoof; it is ceremonially unclean for you. The coney, though it chews the cud, does not have a split hoof; it is unclean for you. The rabbit, though it chews the cud, does not have a split hoof; it is unclean for you. And the pig, though it has a split hoof completely divided, does not chew the cud; it is unclean for you. You must not eat their meat or touch their carcasses; they are unclean for you.

"'Of all the creatures living in the water of the seas and the streams, you may eat any that have fins and scales. But all creatures in the seas or streams that do not have fins and scales – whether among all the swarming things or among all the other living creatures in the water – you are to detest. And since you are to detest them, you must not eat their meat and you must detest their carcasses. Anything living in the water that does not have fins and scales is to be detestable to you. . . .

"'I am the LORD your God; consecrate yourselves and be holy, because I am holy. Do not make yourselves unclean by any creature that moves about on the ground. I am the LORD who brought you up out of Egypt to be your God; therefore be holy, because I am holy.

"'These are the regulations concerning animals, birds, every living thing that moves in the water and every creature that moves about on the ground. You must distinguish between the unclean and the clean, between living creatures that may be eaten and those that may not be eaten.'"

The distinction between clean and unclean animals basically means that "clean" animals could be eaten, but the unclean ones were forbidden food for the Israelites. One of the first questions that is likely to come to our minds is: but *why* are some animals unclean whereas others are clean? Different people have answered this question in many different ways over the years.

1. One answer is that God declared some animals unclean for hygienic or medical reasons. Animals that are unclean are detrimental to people's health. The Jewish doctor Maimonides, who lived in the Middle Ages, gives this reason. "I maintain that food which is forbidden by the Law is unwholesome. There is nothing among the forbidden kinds of food whose injurious character is doubted except for pork and fat; but in these cases also the doubt is not justified."[94]

Some modern biblical commentators use this argument extensively.[95] They argue, for example, that modern research shows that pigs contain many bacteria. This explanation appeals, therefore, to modern people. It sounds like a very rational argument, and many people today are interested in healthy food and living. Does this mean that the argument itself is correct?

The medical reasons would not have been clear to the Israelites at all. We know far more about diseases caused by meat than they did. The list of unclean animals also includes many different animals – and while the Israelites may have known that pigs were not very hygienic animals, what about the camel, the white owl, and the stork?

Another crucial argument against this explanation is that it would be very hard to explain why, if these animals are dangerous to our health, Jesus declared all foods "clean" (Mark 7:19 and Matt. 15:17–20). This explanation, therefore, does not provide the key for understanding the food laws.

2. The second explanation that has been offered is almost the opposite of the first one. It says that there is no rational motive at all. The list of unclean and clean animals is completely arbitrary and was only meant to test the obedience of the people – as some rabbis thought.

Some older scholars say that Leviticus 11 – 15 is one of the most difficult parts of the Old Testament. In their opinion these chapters show only that the priests who wrote them were very rigid-minded to create such regulations. They consider these chapters to be the counterpart to the teaching of the great prophets, who emphasize the inner rather than the outer. All of these explanations are rather negative, and so we look for others.

3. Do the regulations have to do with religious customs? Are they a reaction against other nations, who use some of the unclean animals in their worship of idols?[96] This argument cannot be correct for the simple reason that the bull is the most important cultic animal in Canaanite religion, but according to Leviticus 11 it is not unclean.

4. A very old explanation is that the regulations are meant symbolically: uncleanness is a metaphor for sin. Animals who chew the cud are clean (Lev. 11:3–7, 26), which means that human beings should "chew," or meditate, on the law.

This explanation is first found in the Letter of Aristeas, a Hellenized Jew who probably wrote the letter in the second century BC from Alexandria. The author explains that the winged creatures that are allowed for consumption are feeding on "wheat and pulse," whereas the forbidden ones are "wild and carnivorous":

> By these creatures, then, which he called unclean, the lawgiver gave a sign that those for whom the laws were ordained must practice righteousness in their hearts and oppress no one, trusting in their own strength, nor rob one of anything, but must direct their lives by righteous motives. . . . He has, then, set forth all these rules as to what is permitted us in the case of these and the other creatures by way of allegory. For the parting of the hoof and the dividing of the claws symbolize discrimination in our every action with a view to what is right . . .[97]

The author of the Epistle of Barnabas,[98] which belongs to the so-called Apostolic Fathers, likewise thinks that the animals were not literal animals at all. The rules concerning food are only about spiritual things. The "animals" are people with whom the faithful should not mix:

> The meaning of his allusion to swine is this: what he is really saying is, "you are not to consort with the class of people who are like swine, inasmuch as they forget all about the Lord while they are living in affluence, but remember Him when they are in want . . ."

The epistle offers a similar sort of explanation for each animal. The expression "anything that chews the cud" is equated with "men who fear the Lord." One should seek their company, because they are the ones "who muse in their hearts on the purport of every word they have received . . . who know that meditation is a delight – who do, in fact, *chew the cud* of the Lord's word."[99]

In the nineteenth century this type of allegorizing interpretation occurs, for example, in the *Notes on the Book of Leviticus* from the hand of the Dispensationalist C. H. M. (Charles Mackintosh), who writes:

> The chewing of the cud expresses the natural process of "inwardly digesting" that which one eats; while the divided hoof sets forth the character of one's outward walk. There is, as we know, an intimate connexion between the two, in the christian life. . . . It is feared that many who read the Bible do not digest the word. The two things are widely different.[100]

This allegorical interpretation is unlikely, however, to convince modern people.

5. Contemporary author Jacob Milgrom argues that the list in Leviticus 11 restricts the number of animals to

be eaten and therefore restricts hunting, which was a beloved sport among the nations around Israel.[101] Both the prohibition to consume blood and the rules about clean and unclean animals result in a restriction on hunting and killing God's creatures. Those animals that may be consumed are herbivores. It is not right to eat animals that are hunters and carnivores, but there is no restriction on eating fruit and vegetables. Animals for consumption were usually killed near the sanctuary in a quick and painless way. Deuteronomy 12:20–27 does indeed regulate hunting and eating animals at home.

Milgrom's explanation does shed some light on the interpretation of Leviticus 11. However, we may need to probe deeper still. Milgrom himself acknowledges this by putting the whole system of food laws in the wider context of holiness – being set apart as the people of God.[102]

Edwin Firmage, however, argues that it is unlikely that the forbidden animals would be designated in such a negative way ("detestable," "unclean") if the rules were only meant to express a positive attitude to life. Firmage himself thinks that the list of clean animals includes most of the animals to be sacrificed, and that the list of clean animals is derived from the list of animals that are allowed for sacrifice.[103]

There has been a lot more discussion about this issue, for example in Jenson's and Houston's recent studies.[104] Houston criticizes Firmage's opinion, because the God of Israel is never imagined to "eat sacrifices," as the gods of some other nations do. Therefore Israel cannot copy God in what they eat or do not eat.

None of these explanations, however, seem to touch the heart of what God is saying here in Leviticus 11.

6. The most plausible explanation for the regulations in Leviticus 11 concentrates on this idea of holiness and being set apart. I first encountered this explanation in Wenham's commentary on Leviticus and in a more recent commentary written by John Hartley.[105] Hartley adds an important point to the debate in arguing that life, and not death, belongs to God – an issue Wenham mentions in his later work as well.[106] The issues in Leviticus 11 are important for understanding not only the whole book of Leviticus, but also the special position that the people of Israel had.

In his commentary on Leviticus, Wenham builds on the work of Mary Douglas, who did a lot of social-anthropological research.[107] The main issues in Leviticus 11 concern wholeness, holiness, and integrity. The passage mentions three categories of animals: those walking on land (vv. 1–8), those swimming in water (vv. 9–12) and those flying in the air (vv. 13–23; see Gen. 1:20–30 for the same categories). According to Wenham, who follows Douglas, these categories are all based on a "norm" for locomotion belonging to each of the categories. What is "normal" belongs to the essence of the animal and shows its integrity. Thus it is "normal" that land animals have hooves for running, that fish have fins and scales for swimming and that birds have two wings for flying and two legs for walking. Since such animals are as they should be, they represent the idea of "wholeness" and "integrity."

Douglas' view has been criticized, mainly based on the idea of "motion." Many scholars have accepted Douglas' idea of wholeness as a key concept. To Wenham in *Story as Torah*, the concepts of wholeness, integrity, holiness, and life are most central. In all of the laws, *life*, which belongs to God, is the central issue.[108]

Before we look at this more carefully, let us first investigate the context of Leviticus 11.

Wholeness

We have touched on the issue of "wholeness" in Leviticus 11, which is an important theme in other parts of Leviticus as well. Things that were not "whole," in the sense that they were not "one whole thing" (either of one and the same kind or without fault or disease) were forbidden. Thus we read in Leviticus 19:19: "Do not mate different kinds of animals. Do not plant your field with two kinds of seed. Do not wear clothing woven of two kinds of material."

Wholeness and integrity are very important issues. If someone's skin was infected by a disease, that person was not "whole" and they were considered "unclean" (Lev. 13). Clothing and houses could also become "unclean" by being "contaminated with mildew" (Lev. 13:47–59; 14:33–57). The regulations in Leviticus 15 about losing semen and about menstruation also have to do with "wholeness": losing semen or blood symbolizes losing "life," which is the opposite of the "whole life" which belongs to God and his realm. All of these regulations serve as daily reminders of God's holiness, wholeness, integrity, and of the quality of a "full" life which belongs to God and his people: ". . . be holy, because I am holy" (Lev. 11:44).

Excursus: Sexuality

The uncleanness of a man who loses semen and of a man and woman who have had sexual intercourse does not mean that everything that has to do with sexuality is unclean. The regulations do make clear, however, that sexuality is not a "cultic" thing and that there is no relationship between the temple and sexual conduct. This may sound strange to us, but it is a very important issue in the world in which Israel lived. In Canaan, "cultic prostitution" was quite common, hence the rule of Deuteronomy 23:17: "No Israelite man or woman is to become a shrine-prostitute." In Numbers 25 we read about the same sort of prostitution, which threatened the Israelites' living as the people of God. "While Israel was staying in Shittim, the men began to indulge in sexual immorality with Moabite women, who invited them to the sacrifices to their gods. The people ate and bowed down before these gods. So Israel joined in worshiping the Baal of Peor. And the LORD's anger burned against them" (Num. 25:1–3).[109] Here again, worshiping other gods is mixed with prostitution.

In the city-state of Ugarit, whose religion was close to that of the Canaanites, there was a so-called "sacred marriage" during the New Year's festival. The king was expected to have intercourse with the queen and with a princess, and all three of them represented a god. People thought this would stimulate fertility. During the dry season, the god of fertility stayed in the underworld. The god of death, however, was conquered when the wet season started and the god of fertility came to life again. The king was to "imitate" what happened in the world of the gods, and in this way he initiated the conduct of the gods. Fertility had to be enacted, as it were.[110]

In the book of Hosea, and also at the beginning of the book of Jeremiah, we encounter this way of thinking that threatened Israel's life as the people of God. They were constantly in danger of mixing the worship of the one and only God with that of others. Idolatry and adultery are closely bound together because adultery was part of the worship of Baal – the primary focus of which was fertility.[111]

The rules about cleanness and uncleanness in relation to sexuality make clear that Israel should be different, distinct from other nations. Sexuality is not to be divinized, but it has its own place in creation as a gift from God to a man and a woman (Gen. 2:24).

Three categories

In his commentary on Leviticus, Wenham also explains the distinction in Leviticus 11 between clean animals that God allowed the Israelites to eat and some others that were clean *and* could be used in sacrifices. So, in fact, there are three categories of animals: the unclean, the clean (for food only), and the clean fit for food and sacrifice. Wenham explains the distinction as symbolic of a division of humanity into three categories: the non-Israelites were "unclean," the Israelites were "clean" and the priests were dedicated in a special way to serve God. Wenham concludes that every meal reminded the Israelites of their special position as members of God's chosen people and of their responsibility to serve him wholeheartedly.[112]

Set apart

It is clear from the preceding discussion that it is not a simple matter to know exactly why certain animals were clean and others were not. What is clear, however, is that the regulations are about wholeness, life, integrity, completeness – reflecting the "holiness" of God. As Wenham argues, "God is the source of life and so holiness virtually equates to the life-giving power of God."[113] "But divine holiness does not merely demand total religious and moral commitment, it means life. God himself is full and perfect life, so that death is the very antithesis of holiness."[114]

That God expects his people to reflect his holiness is clear, for example in Leviticus 11:44–45:

> I am the LORD your God; consecrate yourselves and be holy, because I am holy. . . . I am the LORD who brought you up out of Egypt to be your God; therefore be holy, because I am holy.

And Leviticus 20:25–26 states:

> You must therefore make a distinction between clean and unclean animals and between unclean and clean birds. Do not defile yourselves by any animal or bird or anything that moves along the ground – those which I have set apart as unclean for you. You are to be holy to me because I, the LORD, am holy, and I have set you apart from the nations to be my own.

It is clear that we need to consider the context of the whole book of Leviticus in order to gain a better understanding of the food laws in Leviticus 11. The specific regulations on clean and unclean animals reflect the principles behind all of the regulations about cleanness and uncleanness.

We conclude that the food laws illustrated and brought home to the people of Israel that they were "different." They were a people set apart by the Holy One in order to serve him with their whole lives. They were to reflect that separateness in every aspect of their daily lives – in their food and clothing and in their conduct. They had to reflect the wholeness, the completeness, the integrity, holiness, and life of God – because God called them to be like himself. God is the source of life, which is opposite to death. Wholeness is opposite to being "mixed" in your commitment to him – completeness and integrity are opposed to chaos and disintegration. God is the living God; he is the God of life. Milgrom investigates the word "holiness" and emphasizes the aspect of "being set apart from" with a certain purpose. Israel was supposed to be an "image" of God in their way of living – even in the food they ate or would not eat. "Holiness means *imitatio Dei* – the life of godliness."[115]

Leviticus 19

As we said above, God is life and the realm of life and living, order, wholeness, and integrity belong to him. The opposite of life is death, and everything that had to do with death was unclean for the Israelites. Thus anybody who had touched a corpse was unclean. Consulting the dead, a practice widely known in those days, was also forbidden (Deut. 18:9–13). The whole area of forbidden practices such as divination, witchcraft, and spiritism makes the contrast between Israel and other nations clear: "Anyone who does these things is detestable to the LORD, and because of these detestable practices the LORD your God will drive out those nations before you. You must be blameless before the LORD your God" (Deut. 18:12–13).

As we have seen, many of the rules and regulations in the Torah were intended to set Israel apart as the people of God. God forbade them, therefore, to take part in things that played an important role in the worship of other gods.

Leviticus 19 also spells out this idea of distinctiveness in detail. The following words function there as a refrain: "I am the LORD (your God)" (vv. 3, 4, 10, 12, 14, 16, 18, 25, 30, 31, 32, 34, 37). All laws and regulations in the chapter are related to the Giver of the laws, the holy God of Israel. The words "your God" reaffirm the relationship.

The chapter begins by setting out a sort of program for Israel's life: "Be holy because I, the LORD your God, am holy" (v. 1).

As we have established, God's holiness and his people's reflection of that holiness are essential to understanding the laws in Leviticus. Leviticus 19 underlines that the calling of Israel embraces every aspect of life: one's relationship to parents, keeping the Sabbath, offering sacrifices in the right way, justice, honesty, avoiding anything which may harm another person. The chapter even includes the command to "love your neighbor as yourself" (v. 18; see also the New Testament).

These commandments are followed by some regulations about integrity and wholeness, such as not mating different kinds of animals (see above). Some other commands again warn against the practices of other nations, such as divination and cutting the body as a ritual in mourning (vv. 26b–28). God reminds the people of his saving acts at the end of this chapter. This reminder is intended to heighten their motivation for caring for the "aliens" – that is, those non-Israelites who lived permanently in the land but did not own land themselves. These aliens were therefore dependent on the goodness of the Israelites, just as the "widow" and the "fatherless," who are often mentioned together as the most vulnerable groups in society. God reminds the Israelites why they should care for these people in Deuteronomy 24:22: "Remember that you were slaves in Egypt. That is why I command you to do this" (see also vv. 14, 17, 20, 21).

The commands in Leviticus 19 cover every area of life – there is no division between the "religious" and the "secular." Neither can we group the laws according to "moral" and "cultic" divisions – or any other categories.[116]

Conclusions

When we lay the framework of Old Testament ethics as we discovered it in the previous chapters side by side with what we discussed in Leviticus, we identify several important issues:

♦ From Wright's triangle, it is clear that Old Testament ethics is "God-centred." The rules about clean and unclean food were given by God and do not have to be fully understood by human beings. The crucial point was that the Israelites responded to them with obedience.
♦ Basically the laws have a paradigmatic function, for by keeping them the people reflect God's wholeness and holiness and their distinctiveness from the other nations. By keeping God's commandments Israel shows to the world what it means to be God's people.
♦ Old Testament ethics is based on God's grace; both Leviticus 11:45 and chapter 19 refer to God's deliverance of the Israelites from slavery.
♦ The "theocentric" character of the commandments also means that they apply to all of life in its fullness, for God is the Giver of life.

- There is no strict division between "spiritual" and "physical" areas of life, or between the "horizontal" and the "vertical." God wants his people to live all of their lives in the light of his presence. Old Testament ethics is therefore a *way of living*.

Based on Leviticus 19 we can also add that:

- The land plays an important role in Israel's history (see, e.g., Lev. 19:9, 19, 23–25, 29).
- Ethics in the Old Testament is not (only) about individuals, but (also) about community: Leviticus 19 refers frequently to "your neighbor" – whether that means the blind, the poor, one's parents or someone else.

Questions for further reflection

1. How would you describe "holiness"?
2. How could we structure our worship in order to emphasize God's holiness more effectively?
3. How can the principle of wholeness be applied to our lives as Christians?

5

Canceling Debts: Applying the Framework

The Torah includes regulations on different occasions regarding a year of rest for the land, the so-called Sabbath year, every seventh year. In Deuteronomy 15:1–11 we find rules about the cancellation of debts during this special Sabbath year:

At the end of every seven years you must cancel debts. This is how it is to be done: Every creditor shall cancel the loan he has made to his fellow Israelite. He shall not require payment from his fellow Israelite or brother, because the Lord's time for canceling debts has been proclaimed. You may require payment from a foreigner, but you must cancel any debt your brother owes you. However, there should be no poor among you, for in the land the Lord your God is giving you to possess as your inheritance, he will richly bless you, if only you fully obey the Lord your God and are careful to follow all these commands I am giving you today. For the Lord your God will bless you as he has promised, and you will lend to many nations but will borrow from none. You will rule over many nations but none will rule over you.

> If there is a poor man among your brothers in any of the towns of the land that the LORD your God is giving you, do not be hardhearted or tightfisted toward your poor brother. Rather be openhanded and freely lend him whatever he needs. Be careful not to harbor this wicked thought: "The seventh year, the year for canceling debts, is near," so that you do not show ill will toward your needy brother and give him nothing. He may then appeal to the LORD against you, and you will be found guilty of sin. Give generously to him and do so without a grudging heart; then because of this the LORD your God will bless you in all your work and in everything you put your hand to. There will always be poor people in the land. Therefore I command you to be openhanded toward your brothers and toward the poor and needy in your land.

Every seventh year was a Sabbath year, during which the land was to lay fallow. Any food that grew spontaneously was to be given to the poor. Just like the weekly Sabbath, this year was meant to be a time of rest. Not only were the landowners meant to be resting, but also those who worked for them – humans and animals alike. The Sabbath day of rest has the social benefit of a day off for people and animals who are working hard. Exodus 20:8–11 refers to God's work of creation as a motivation for keeping the Sabbath day. The Sabbath year has the same value.

Exodus 23:10–12 describes the Sabbath and the Sabbath year in terms of their social and physical benefits.

> For six years you are to sow your fields and harvest the crops, but during the seventh year let the land lie unplowed and unused. Then the poor among your people may get food from it, and the wild animals may eat what

they leave. Do the same with your vineyard and your olive grove.

Six days do your work, but on the seventh day do not work, so that your ox and your donkey may rest and the slave born in your household, and the alien as well, may be refreshed.

God – land – people

Another passage with regulations regarding the Sabbath year, Leviticus 25, emphasizes a period of rest for the land. Here the poor are not mentioned. In Deuteronomy 15:1–11, however, the emphasis is on canceling the debts of the poor. We look in particular at the social implications of the Sabbath year. All three angles of Wright's triangle are important for our understanding of these laws. First of all, the law of Deuteronomy 15:1–11 is about God, "God-centred." It is "the LORD's time for canceling debts" (v. 2); the land is given by the LORD your God (vv. 4, 7); "the LORD your God will bless you" (vv. 6, 10). The commands which need to be obeyed are God's (v. 5). The law regarding the cancelation of debts is put in the context of "the LORD your God," which is a reminder of the covenant at Sinai. Israel is God's people, and obeying his commands is part of living in a special relationship with him. He gives this law, and keeping it or failing to keep it influences Israel's relationship with him.

Furthermore, there is a relationship between this God-given command, the land, and the neighbor, or brother. In particular, the word "to bless" is important here. Verse 10 states that God will bless his people in all their work if they keep his law. If Israel simply obeyed God's laws there should not be poor people in the land, because God promises to bless them richly if they obey him. However, the reality will be that there are poor people (vv. 7, 11), and therefore these regulations are necessary.

Verse 1 gives the rule in brief, and verses 2–11 tell the people how to live out the rule. In the seventh year, the debts of a fellow Israelite or a brother (basically one and the same) should be canceled. The word "your" (brother) makes things very personal. The other person is not far away – he is my brother. Verse 11 makes this point very clearly. "Therefore I command you to be openhanded toward your brothers and toward the poor and needy in your land." The word "your" is used twice. It is "my" business that there are poor people in "my" land. God's people live in relationship with him *and* with one another.

What about the "foreigner" in verse 3? Is he not to be treated with the same respect as a fellow Israelite? That is not the intended meaning. The "foreigner" was someone who did not live in the land permanently, but who came on a regular basis to do business. As such, foreigners did not take part in the Sabbath year and could earn money as usual, so they could pay their debts as usual. The "alien" in the Old Testament is a different kind of person.[117]

What does "cancelation of debts" mean? Some scholars think that it means postponement of payment. Yet a *total* cancellation seems to be a more plausible explanation than mere postponement of payment if we take into account the fact that the weekly "Sabbath" was meant as a day of *total* rest. The next passage, Deuteronomy 15:12–18, gives the instruction that slaves are to be released after six years of service, unless they prefer to stay. It would therefore seem to follow that Deuteronomy 15:1–11 mandates a "total release" of debts.

The passage as a whole demonstrates that an attitude of wholehearted cancellation is required, and verses 7–11 emphasize this point. If a poor person wants to borrow from somebody else who owns more than he does, the response should be "openhanded" and the request granted "freely" (v. 8).[118] The logical thought: "I'd better not give him anything, because the year for canceling debts is near and I won't get my money back," is called a "wicked" thought (v. 9). Literally, in Hebrew, it is "a thought or word of Belial." The word "Belial" means without any use, worthless. It describes things or persons considered "worthless," causing chaos and destruction. So, for example, the sons of Eli are called "sons of Belial" (1 Sam. 2:12, KJV; cf. the note in NASB). Sin causes chaos and destroys good relationships between God and people.[119]

The opposite of the selfish thought of restraining from giving is a form of giving which is "openhanded." God has given the people the good promised land, full of blessings. This land is Israel's heritage and a gift from the LORD their God. It is therefore meant to be part of the life of every Israelite, and not just of the rich, the lucky or the skillful. Each member of the covenant people could have their share in the inheritance God had given. Even when they were so unlucky as to lose their land, it had to be given back to them, as we read in Leviticus 25, the regulations concerning the so-called Year of Jubilee.

Leviticus 25 combines the rules and regulations regarding the Sabbath year with those about the Year of Jubilee. After seven cycles of seven years (or after seven Sabbath years), there is a fiftieth year called the Year of Jubilee. Leviticus 25:10b prescribes: ". . . each one of you is to return to his family property and each to his own clan." People were released from debts, land that they had lost was returned to them and slaves were set free.

The chapter as a whole concerns Israelites who worked as slaves for someone else because they hadn't been able to pay their debts.[120]

Israelites should not rule over other Israelites "ruthlessly," according to Leviticus 25:43. The theological motivation for this command is that God freed the Israelites from slavery in Egypt to be *his* servants. Israelites were not meant to be slaves of other human beings, and in particular not of fellow-Israelites (Lev. 25:42–43, 55). The covenant people should not be divided into a ruling class and a class of exploited servants.

In Babylonian society slaves belonged to the lowest class and were regarded as possessions. If a slave ran away and was helped by someone who gave him refuge, that person had to be killed.[121] According to Deuteronomy 23:15–16, however, a runaway slave who finds refuge should not be handed back to his master. Regulations in the Torah on slaves and slavery are mild in comparison to those in other writings from the ancient Near East, even though some of them are quite similar.

In the Old Testament, a master who hit his slave so that he died had to be punished (Exod. 21:20). In the law book of Hammurabi (par. 116) we find a rule about the death of someone who worked for another person because he was in debt. If his master beat him so that he died, the master's punishment depended on the sort of status the slave had: if he came from a family of slaves, the only punishment was paying a fine. But if the slave had been the son of a free man, then the son (!) of the master who hit him had to be killed.[122] The sort of rule we find in Exodus 21:26–27 is completely foreign to the law book of Hammurabi:

If a man hits a manservant or maidservant in the eye and destroys it, he must let the servant go free to compensate

for the eye. And if he knocks out the tooth of a manservant
or maidservant, he must let the servant go free to compensate for the tooth.

The Old Testament view was that a slave was a person
with his own rights. Hans Boecker remarks: "He has
rights of his own, particularly the right to bodily integrity."[123]

The events related in Jeremiah 34 remind us of the
regulations regarding the freeing of slaves. King
Zedekiah, who is in danger because the Babylonians
have surrounded Jerusalem, agreed that the rich should
release their slaves. He expected that, if he started to
keep the law on the release of slaves, this obedience
would result in deliverance from their enemies. The
slaves were freed and, indeed, the Babylonians with-
drew. At that moment, however, the rich took back their
slaves. This is obviously not how the law was meant to
be applied. Jeremiah received a word from God proclaiming severe judgement on the slave owners: they
would be owned by the Babylonians. They would be
"set free" to fall by the sword, plague and famine (Jer.
34:17b).[124]

The intended result of the Sabbath year and the Year
of Jubilee was that the original situation in the land
would be restored. Someone who had debts could make
a fresh start, as if he had never had any debts at all. Land
would be returned to the original owner or family.
Behind these rules, again, is the idea that the land was
the inheritance given to the covenant people as a whole.
Each individual Israelite should enjoy his share. Land
was necessary for income and for life and consequently
had to stay within the family. That is why there are also
rules about the redemption of land by a member of the
family (Lev. 25:23–25). Jeremiah 32 gives an example of

such redemption. Jeremiah receives a command from God to buy a piece of land from the son of his uncle so that this land will stay in the family.

We do not know whether or not Israel kept the Year of Jubilee. But it is obvious that it was not kept regularly – otherwise the Historical and Prophetic Books would have referred to its observance. Leviticus 26:34, 43 and 2 Chronicles 36:21 connect the failure to keep the Year of Jubilee with the number of years of the exile: during a period of exile the land will finally lie fallow. In 2 Kings 25:12 we read that the commander of the Babylonians, while carrying the most important Judean people into exile, "left behind some of the poorest people of the land to work the vineyards and fields." In this unexpected way, the poor still received the share of the land they should have received before.

Despite the legislation in the Torah, a clear distinction between rich and poor people developed in Israel. This is already evident when Solomon uses people to realize his building plans. In 1 Kings 9:22 we read that the Israelites had not been made slaves, in contrast with people from the nations who were still left in Canaan (vv. 20–21). But after Solomon's death it became clear that Israelites, too, had had heavy burdens during his reign (1 Kgs. 12:4).

From the words of the prophets we know that the rich exploited the poor. The prophets openly and strongly protested against this. Micah, for example, proclaimed:

Woe to those who plan iniquity, to those who plot evil on their beds!
At morning's light they carry it out because it is in their power to do it.

They covet fields and seize them, and houses, and take them.
They defraud a man of his home, a fellowman of his inheritance (Micah 2:1–2).

Conclusions

+ As we have seen again and again, Old Testament ethics is "God-centred." It is the "Lord your God" who gives the law to his covenant people, it is he who blesses them and who therefore provides everything necessary to obey his commands.
+ The way Israel deals with the land and poverty should be an example, a paradigm, of what God's world is meant to look like. There is blessing for everyone and there should be no poor people.
+ Old Testament ethics is based on God's grace: he has given the land and he gives blessings to his people.
+ The "theocentric" character of the commandments also means that they have to do with life in its fullness, for God is the Giver of life.
+ There is no strict division between a "spiritual" and a "physical" life. The whole of life, including the realm of economics, is meant to be lived in the light of God's presence. Old Testament ethics is a *way of living*. One shows that he or she serves God by keeping his commandments – and this obedience will result in blessing for the land and even in the lifting of poverty.
+ The land plays an important role in Israel's history. We saw this clearly in Wright's triangle, as well as in Deuteronomy 15:1–11.
+ Ethics in the Old Testament is not (only) about individuals, but about community.

In the final chapter we will consider some implications of Deuteronomy 15:1–11 for the New Testament church.

Questions for further reflection

1. Who are the "aliens," the "widows," and the "orphans" in our society? And how can we as Christians fulfill the Old Testament mandate to care for them?
2. Does it make any difference whether you have experienced "slavery" yourself or not? How is the way you treat others influenced by what you have experienced yourself?

6

Warfare: Applying the Framework

Not a few Christians argue that the Old Testament is not for them because it is a book full of wars and violence. Is that a correct impression? Is the Old Testament full of wars? How does it discuss warfare?

In the first place, we might make a distinction between the biblical ideal and what actually happened. In this study we are primarily concerned with the ideal. What commandments, which ethical values did God give to his people? Whether or not Israel kept these commandments is a separate issue. As Wenham remarks, "It is evident that neither Genesis nor Judges [the books he deals with in particular] holds up all the actions of its actors as admirable, but that God acts in grace towards his fallible people."[125]

How can we conceive of God thinking about warfare? Can a God who gives laws on warfare also be a God who is love? Is the Old Testament indeed totally different from the New Testament, where Jesus says: "Love your enemies"? We actually need to ask whether the New Testament is indeed a "pacifist" book. New Testament passages about the future use much language derived from battle (see, e.g., Mark 13:7, Rev. 6:3–8; 19:11–21). We will return to this question in the final chapter.

Some theologians argue that the rules on warfare are basically the product of one or more theological sources in Israel, and that they can be considered as simply the opinions of these particular groups of redactors or authors. Some of the laws, they claim, stem from a strict group of people who were proclaiming war against foreign influences.[126] On this basis one could say that the Old Testament just contains different attitudes to, and opinions on, warfare.[127] These scholars conclude that different passages are merely the work of human beings and that, therefore, they have less authority than God's revelation and are less of a problem.

But if we believe that God reveals himself in his word, it is very important to listen to the texts themselves before we pronounce judgement. We will first take a closer look at Deuteronomy 20:

> When you go to war against your enemies and see horses and chariots and an army greater than yours, do not be afraid of them, because the LORD your God, who brought you up out of Egypt, will be with you. When you are about to go into battle, the priest shall come forward and address the army. He shall say: "Hear, O Israel, today you are going into battle against your enemies. Do not be fainthearted or afraid; do not be terrified or give way to panic before them. For the LORD your God is the one who goes with you to fight for you against your enemies to give you victory."
>
> The officers shall say to the army: "Has anyone built a new house and not dedicated it? Let him go home, or he may die in battle and someone else may dedicate it. Has anyone planted a vineyard and not begun to enjoy it? Let him go home, or he may die in battle and someone else enjoy it. Has anyone become pledged to a woman and not married her? Let him go home, or he may die in battle and someone

else marry her." Then the officers shall add, "Is any man afraid or fainthearted? Let him go home so that his brothers will not become disheartened too." When the officers have finished speaking to the army, they shall appoint commanders over it.

When you march up to attack a city, make its people an offer of peace. If they accept and open their gates, all the people in it shall be subject to forced labor and shall work for you. If they refuse to make peace and they engage you in battle, lay siege to that city. When the LORD your God delivers it into your hand, put to the sword all the men in it. As for the women, the children, the livestock and everything else in the city, you may take these as plunder for yourselves. And you may use the plunder the LORD your God gives you from your enemies. This is how you are to treat all the cities that are at a distance from you and do not belong to the nations nearby.

However, in the cities of the nations the LORD your God is giving you as an inheritance, do not leave alive anything that breathes. Completely destroy them – the Hittites, Amorites, Canaanites, Perizzites, Hivites and Jebusites – as the LORD your God has commanded you. Otherwise, they will teach you to follow all the detestable things they do in worshiping their gods, and you will sin against the LORD your God.

When you lay siege to a city for a long time, fighting against it to capture it, do not destroy its trees by putting an axe to them, because you can eat their fruit. Do not cut them down. Are the trees of the field people, that you should besiege them? However, you may cut down trees that you know are not fruit trees and use them to build siege works until the city at war with you falls.

Israel in its context

Deuteronomy presents itself as a long sermon given by Moses just before the people of Israel enter the promised land of Canaan. Deuteronomy 20 gives regulations about what Israel should do when they encounter other peoples in the land or when they are attacked by other nations. The passage is not about conquering as many foreign countries and nations as possible. Warfare is not glorified.

Some scholars think that Deuteronomy 20 was written a long time after the conquest of Canaan, and they date the law on warfare from the time of the monarchy. T. Raymond Hobbs argues that Deuteronomy 20, 21 and 23 mention foreign nations that are relevant in the time of the kings, when warfare had become more aggressive than it was in earlier times.[128] Deuteronomy 20 does not promote aggressive warfare at all, as we will see – although Hobbs interprets the chapter more negatively. Wright is able to defend a much earlier date for the passage and explains it as a rule that was indeed given before the conquest of the land. He argues that it made no sense for these rules to be written down at a later time when everybody knew they were not kept.[129]

Israel had to deal with several great kingdoms during its Old Testament history. These kingdoms in turn tried to expand their realms at the expense of other nations such as Israel. Geographically, the land of Canaan was situated between some mighty powers: Egypt on one side, and Assyria and later Babylonia on the other. For a long time there was an ongoing struggle for supremacy between the great power to Israel's west and that in the northeast. Whenever these powers wanted to attack each other, they passed through Israel's land.

Warfare was a more or less common reality in the ancient Near East. Some powers, like Assyria, did not have natural fixed borders such as coastlines. The Assyrians were therefore quite vulnerable and were constantly on the move to secure their kingdom and their realm against invaders.

The Assyrians are often pictured as a ruthless, cruel people without any respect for human life. In their writings and in the reliefs showing their methods of warfare, there are examples of conquered people taken away into captivity. Some captives were skinned alive, others were beheaded. There are reliefs depicting houses being destroyed and burned. The Assyrians were particularly ruthless towards nations that did not surrender to them of their own accord.

Not all Assyrian kings, however, were imperialistic. There was more warfare during certain periods than others. The way in which the Assyrians described and pictured themselves was also meant for "psychological warfare." They wanted other nations to believe that they were an extremely cruel and powerful nation, so that they would immediately surrender. Out of fear, other peoples would give money and other treasures in order to avoid an Assyrian attack.

These mitigating remarks are not made to suggest that the Assyrians did not fight cruel wars. One of their motives for fighting wars was economic in nature. After each conquest they carried away rich treasures from the conquered country. A remarkable aspect of their warfare was the deportation of people. They used these captives in enormous building projects in Assyria, but deportation was also a means of spreading people in order to avoid rebellion.[130]

Warfare in Israel

The rules for warfare in Deuteronomy differ from the standard practices of the day in at least one important

respect: there is no command to expand the land by conquering the territories of surrounding nations – there is
no motive for imperialistic warfare. Israel does not need
to conquer the rest of the world to prove the greatness of
the Lord. Israel is not meant to become a leading world
power such as the Assyrians themselves, and others,
thought they were meant to be.

Because wars were a reality in everyday life, Israel
had to defend the land they had been given. If people
did not defend their own territory, they would lose it.
Israel was not a "spiritual" entity, but a physical and
political one – real people in a real land that was often on
the "shopping list" of other powers who also wanted to
possess that land.

Yet the rules about warfare in Deuteronomy 20 are
very restrictive. In verse 1 it becomes clear that Israel's
might is not in horses, chariots, and big armies – all of
which were very important in the warfare of other
nations. Israel is not to be a superior power that can
oppress others. They were, in fact, "the fewest of all peoples" (Deut. 7:7) and they would have to find their
strength in God.

Secondly, verse 1 states that Israel's war is God's "business," so to speak. Warfare is not about their power; it is
about the land God has given them. He is fighting against
their enemies (see v. 4). Furthermore, there are rules about
possible reduction of the number of soldiers. Applying
these rules will cause the Israelite army to shrink instead
of grow. This is quite a remarkable attitude towards going
to war! If a man is newly married, or has a new house or
has just planted a vineyard, let him enjoy these blessings
that God has given in the promised land. Is anybody
afraid or fainthearted? Let him go home.[131]

All of this makes it very clear that victory will not be
won because of Israel's human might and power, but

because the Lord is with them. The human role in wars is not glorified.

Verses 10–18 set out a distinction between cities at a distance and those nearby – or the cities of the peoples in Canaan. Genesis 15:16 says regarding one of those peoples, the Amorites, that they were driven out of the land because of their wickedness. After his promise to Abraham concerning the land, God had given peoples like the Amorites some time to change and to convert, but now their sin has "reached its full measure." Concerning other nations in Canaan, Deuteronomy 9:4 says:

> After the LORD your God has driven them out before you, do not say to yourself, "The LORD has brought me here to take possession of this land because of my righteousness." No, it is on account of the wickedness of these nations that the LORD is going to drive them out before you.

Set apart

In addition to judging the peoples in Canaan for their sin, there is another motive behind the strict rules about driving them out of the land: they are a danger to Israel because of their idolatry (Deut. 20:18). If Israel does not completely destroy these people, this is what will happen: "Otherwise, they will teach you to follow all the detestable things they do in worshiping their gods, and you will sin against the LORD your God." The leading principle behind the rules in verses 16–18 about the extinction of Canaanite peoples is that Israel needs to do away with everything that may cause them to turn away from God and sin.

In Deuteronomy 7:1–6 and 25–26 we come across the same motive for fighting the other nations in the

land. Following other religions is the complete opposite of serving the LORD God – and would therefore
endanger Israel's existence as the people of God. This
danger is also the reason that God forbids marriages
between Israelites and others (Deut. 7:3–4). Idolatry
would inevitably creep into such relationships. Israel
had to be totally committed to God and serve him
wholeheartedly. As Deuteronomy 7:6 says, "For you
are a people holy to the LORD your God. The LORD
your God has chosen you out of all the peoples on the
face of the earth to be his people, his treasured possession."

If Israel loses its identity because they have served
other gods, they will lose their existence – they will
stop being the people of God or a people at all. War
against the Canaanites is therefore not a matter of
imperialism, hatred or cruelty. It is, rather, about Israel
preserving its identity as a people committed to the one
and only God.

Humane

Israel was to offer peace to cities at a distance before anything else happened (Deut. 20:10). If these cities
answered in a positive way, they could remain in their
own land and be subject to Israel. They were not to be ill-
treated. If, however, they refused to make peace, Israel
was to go to battle.

The end of Deuteronomy 20 sets out some rules, the
continuing relevance of which goes without saying: in
times of war fruit trees were not to be destroyed or cut
down to be used for siege works. This decree is in
marked contrast with the custom of the Assyrians. When
a city did not submit to them, they would usually

withdraw and burn and destroy the harvest, the trees, and the houses of the surrounding areas.[132]

In Deuteronomy 21:10–14 we find some humane regulations concerning captive women. If an Israelite married such a woman, he was not allowed to sell her or treat her as a slave if he were no longer pleased with her. He was to respect her as a valuable human being.

In this context it is worth looking at the way some of the other nations, except the Canaanites, were treated. Deuteronomy 2 lists three nations to which God had given land – all of which have a historic relationship with Israel. In the case of Edom the connection is through Esau, whose descendants are the people of Edom. Israel is not allowed to fight against Edom or take any of their land, because God has given it to the descendants of Esau (vv. 4–6). The same applies to Moab (v. 9) and to Ammon (v. 19) – nations that are related to Israel through Lot, Abraham's nephew.

Deuteronomy 23:3–8 discusses whether other nations were to be allowed into the assembly of God. The answer to this question depends on how a given nation had treated Israel in the past. The king of Moab had wanted to curse Israel through Balaam, and the Ammonites had hindered Israel on their journey to the promised land. Neither of these nations, therefore, could belong to the assembly of Israel. Edom, however, is related to Israel through Esau, and the Egyptians offered hospitality to Jacob and his family. It is a more distant past, and not Egypt's recent history, that is remembered here. Rather than being strict, these rules are in fact very open-minded towards other nations. The assessment of these other peoples depends on their attitude towards and relationship with Israel. If they are positive towards her, they will share in her blessings (see also Gen. 12:3).

Reality

We said above that there is a difference between the theory of the law and what happened in reality. Did Israel actually keep these regulations on warfare?

1 Kings 9:20–21 makes it clear that Israel did not keep the command to extinguish the Canaanites. This may come as a relief to modern readers, but the downside of it was that the Baal worship of the Canaanites was always a threat to Israel's faith and (therefore) to their existence as the people of God.

There is no simple answer to the question of whether Israel always fought its wars in a humane way. What actually happened during wars is largely unknown to us. We do read, however, that the officials of Benhadad, the king of Aram, say: "Look, we have heard that the kings of the house of Israel are merciful" (1 Kgs. 20:31).

The Bible is also honest about the failures of Israel's kings. Even an "ideal" king like David is not pictured as blameless. It is striking to read in 1 Chronicles 28:3 that David was not allowed to build the temple because he had shed blood. This remark is all the more striking because the books of Chronicles clearly support David's kingship. Among other nations like the Assyrians and the Babylonians, a warrior like David would have been greatly admired on the basis of his success in battle. But the fact that, as a warrior, David is not permitted to build the temple fits with Deuteronomy 20, the law about warfare. The ideal situation is not war, but peace. The ideal king is not the king who fights and conquers other peoples' land. Several prophecies about the future picture a situation of peace when swords will be turned into "plowshares" and spears into "pruning hooks," and the nations will not "train for war anymore" (Isa. 2:4 and Micah 4:3).

Most prophets in the Old Testament consider the might of the great powers of their days to be relative. Everyone who sees pictures of the sort of weaponry the Egyptians had can imagine how impressive Isaiah's words were:[133]

> Woe to those who go down to Egypt for help, who rely on horses,
> who trust in the multitude of their chariots and in the great strength of their horsemen,
> but do not look to the Holy One of Israel, or seek help from the LORD. . . .
> But the Egyptians are men and not God; their horses are flesh and not spirit.
> When the LORD stretches out his hand, he who helps will stumble, he who is helped will fall; both will perish together. (Isa. 31:1, 3)

The people of God needed courage to trust God, who is invisible, while the impressive military powers were present and threatening.

The king

Assyrian kings often referred to themselves, throughout their numerous texts, as "strong king, king of the universe." They boasted in their glorious conquests of other nations and places, and in the wars they undertook in the name of their gods.[134] Albert Grayson describes the Assyrian royal inscriptions: "The motivation for the composition of the royal inscriptions was glorification of the monarch. Despite the strong religious overtones of the royal inscriptions, the centre of each is the king."[135]

Elsewhere, Grayson refers to a text of Tiglath-Pileser I in which, after typically introducing himself as "king of the universe, king of Assyria," Tiglath-Pileser says: "The god Ashur and the great gods . . . commanded me to extend the border of their land."[136]

The enormous statues of themselves that some of these ancient Near Eastern kings had erected, like those in Egypt, also testify to how important they thought themselves to be. The kings of Israel and Judah, however, had a very different God-given role. No royal statues of these kings have been found. Deuteronomy 17:14–20 contains some regulations about kingship in Israel. If Israel decided to have a king, which was apparently not inevitable, the king would have to be chosen by God. Their king was to be different from kings of other nations: he should not gain excessive power or riches or have many wives. The one thing he should do is write for himself a copy of the law of Moses and read in it "all the days of his life" (vv. 18–19). He was as dependent on God's law as anybody else was and should not consider himself any better than his brothers (vv. 19–20). From God's perspective, the king is merely the first among equals. Deuteronomy 17 pictures a king without much power or might, who was truly a servant of God and his people. The ideal king in Israel is not a warrior and, compared to other nations, kingship in Israel is a rather modest affair. McConville emphasizes the fact that the role of the king in Israel was rather restricted, in particular according to the book of Deuteronomy:

> It is clear that Deuteronomy aims to circumscribe the powers of the king (17:14–20). The king, furthermore, has no essential place in the picture built up in Deut. 16:18 – 18:22, and may be appointed only at the request of the people (17:14–15; cf. 28:36). Unlike other ancient kings, he does not fight battles, maintain a harem, or even acquire wealth.[137]

Wars were not fought to glorify the king of Israel or to promote nationalism. The prophets were in a position to critically assess the king, and the nation could even be expelled from the land if they disobeyed God's laws. In Israel, therefore, in contrast to the surrounding nations, God, the king, the nation, and the land were not automatically in alliance. It is interesting to note that Israel was not led out of Egypt by a warrior-king but by a prophet – and it was God who fought for them.[138]

All of this implies that the criteria used to evaluate kings in the Old Testament were very different from the criteria used in the surrounding world. A clear example of this is the biblical description of King Omri. 1 Kings 16:21–27 mentions Omri very briefly, and the evaluation of his rule is negative: "But Omri did evil in the eyes of the LORD and sinned more than all those before him" (1 Kgs. 16:25). It seems strange, therefore, that long after Omri's death the Assyrians still referred to the house of Israel as "the house of Omri." Although this implies that Omri was an important person in the political world of his day, the biblical record hardly mentions his achievements. The royal inscriptions of Assyrian kings, glorifying all of their accomplishments, stand in sharp contrast to this treatment.

The monarchy was an ambivalent issue throughout Israel's history. While God could work through the person of the king, like David, the kings often caused the people to commit idolatry. In time, King Solomon became the sort of king Deuteronomy 17:17 warns against. He acquired great wealth and took many wives from foreign countries, and they led him to serve other gods (1 Kgs. 11:1–8). The division of the kingdom after Solomon's death was God's judgement for his sins (1 Kgs. 11:9–13).

Conclusions

The laws on warfare present several issues for Old
Testament ethics.

+ Ethics is related to that which is given by God in his
  grace. He has given the land to be inherited by his
  people and therefore he will fight for them. Even this
  law on warfare is issued in the context of what God
  gives to his people.
+ We have seen that God's laws and commands reveal
  his ideal for this world. Does this also apply to the
  laws on warfare? In this case we deal with a broken
  world. The Bible never describes war as an ideal that
  kings should engage in to advance their career and
  improve their image. Deuteronomy 20 clearly states
  that distant nations should first be offered peace. Thus
  imperialism could not be part of the mindset of the
  king or the people. Israel's strength was not to be
  found in human military power.

A different set of rules applied to peoples who lived in
Canaan, who because of their idolatry were a danger to
Israel as the people of God. Throughout the Old Testament,
God's ideal for his people is that they would live in peace in
the promised land, with each member of the covenant people enjoying the fruit of the land. The prophets depict such
an ideal future. In the broken world in which Israel lives,
however, the ideal can only be achieved by radically remov-
ing everything that contradicts God and his law. The
ultimate purpose of driving out the Canaanites is not
destroying human beings, but rather getting rid of that
which threatens Israel as the people of God. The "plant" of
idolatry should be uprooted in order to prevent it from
growing and overwhelming God's covenant people.

- The picture of Israel's king in Deuteronomy 17 and the restriction of military power in Deuteronomy 20 are paradigmatic. A great army is not the ideal, and neither is imperialism. Israel's humane treatment of distant nations is also meant to be a model.

- Old Testament ethics is "God-centred." The laws on warfare do not focus on the power of human beings, but rather on God who is the Lord of Israel and King of all nations, which he governs as well (Deut. 2). Ethics is all about him and how to worship him wholeheartedly without being driven away by idolatry.

- There is no strict division between "spiritual" and "physical" matters. Israel's faith in God was even meant to control the way in which they fought their wars.

- Again, we see that the land plays an important role in Israel's life as the people of God. This law on warfare deals specifically with the possession of the land.

Questions for further reflection

1. Is it possible to have a "just war"? Why or why not?
2. How could the fact that the twentieth century was an age full of war be used in dialogue with Christians who find the Old Testament a hard book to accept?

7

The Old and the New Testament – The Church

Having worked through a framework for looking at the principles behind Old Testament ethics, in this chapter we will turn to the question of contemporary relevance. We have already seen that Christians differ in their views on the relevance and use of Old Testament commands and laws in the church today.[139] We begin by looking at the relationship between the Old and New Testaments.

The relationship between the Old and the New Testaments

The New Testament itself discusses the relevance of the laws given in what would come to be known as the Old Testament. The Old Testament tells the story of the people of Israel and the history of God with people before Christ's coming. The New Testament deals with Jews and non-Jews who believe in Jesus Christ. From the beginning of the Christian movement, one of the fundamental questions was whether the laws of Moses should apply to these non-Jewish believers as well. In other words, is the new covenant, initiated by Jesus, so "new" that the old covenant is now out of date and irrelevant? Were not the requirements facing believers in both eras radically different?

In the second century, a person named Marcion taught that the god of the Old Testament was a different god from the God of the New Testament. The first was a "cruel" god, the second a God of love. Marcion taught that the Old Testament was a book from the past and irrelevant for Christians. The canon could do without it. Not many Christians agree with Marcion, but in practice many do have problems with the Old Testament.

Another discontinuity that lurks in the minds of Bible readers is that developed by Luther, namely that of law (Old Testament) versus grace (New Testament). Dispensationalists, for example, tend towards this position by dividing history into several "dispensations."[140]

In the more recent history of the church, different theologians have developed a variety of views on the Old Testament.[141] The influential German scholar Rudolf Bultmann, for example, thought of the Old Testament as a history of failure – showing how Israel had missed the chance to live according to God's plan. The Dutch scholar Arnold van Ruler, however, argued that the Old Testament contains everything that is essential to the Christian faith; the New Testament just explains it a bit more.[142]

Although we cannot address all of the hermeneutical questions about the relationship between the two Testaments in this brief study, we can extract some guiding thoughts from our study thus far to help us better understand the relationship. First of all, there are some essential differences between the Old and New Testaments.

The Old Testament in the New Testament

The New Testament says that several things have now been fulfilled in Jesus Christ and belong to the old covenant, in contrast to the new covenant. One clear example of this is the sacrificial system. The author of the Letter to the Hebrews emphasizes again and again that the sacrifice of Jesus Christ on the cross brought, once and for all, the forgiveness of sins. Jesus' sacrifice is perfect, and no other sacrifices are necessary (Heb. 10:12, 14, 18). Consequently, Christians have free access to God and are no longer dependent on an earthly priest to make sacrifices on their behalf (Heb. 9:7; 10:19). The author says that the sacrifices under the old covenant were "external regulations applying until the time of the new order" (Heb. 9:10).

This means that a new light is also shed on the place where, in Old Testament times, the sacrifices were made – initially the tabernacle and later the temple. Jesus "went through the greater and more perfect tabernacle that is not man-made" (Heb. 9:11, see also v. 24).

This does not mean that the Old Testament no longer has anything to say to us. On the contrary, the author of Hebrews explains that studying Israel's history, including the laws, clarifies Jesus Christ's work and his position on earth and in heaven. The Old Testament makes it clear that Christ is the mediator of the new covenant (Heb. 9:15), that he is the perfect sacrifice (7:27; 9:26–28; 10:10) and the perfect high priest (4:14; 6:20; 7:28). Many Old Testament institutions point forward to Jesus Christ; they foreshadowed the Light of the world. The laws relating to them are not just abrogated – they are fulfilled.

Food laws

The New Testament explicitly picks up the laws regarding clean and unclean food in Mark 7 and Acts 10. In the latter chapter, the apostle Peter receives a vision while he is praying. Peter's vision plays an important role in the conversion of Cornelius, a non-Jew who is waiting for the Jew Peter to visit him – before Peter is even aware of it. Jews and non-Jews lived separately and could not have a meal together because of the Jewish regulations regarding clean and unclean food. In Peter's vision he sees something like a large sheet with all kinds of clean and unclean animals which he is ordered to eat. Peter refuses, however, because as a Jew faithfully following the rules of the law he had never eaten anything unclean. But a voice instructs him: "Do not call anything impure that God has made clean" (Acts 10:15).

After he sees this vision, some men arrive to bring Peter to the house of a non-Jew. There Peter shows that he has understood what God wanted to say to him, for when he sees Cornelius he says: "You are well aware that it is against our law for a Jew to associate with a Gentile or visit him. But God has shown me that I should not call any man impure or unclean" (Acts 10:28).

This story highlights certain parallels between clean and unclean animals and Jews and Gentiles. As we have seen, the food laws had to do with Israel being set apart as the people of God. Israel's role as model, or paradigm, included their diet. The story in Acts makes clear that, in Jesus Christ, there are no longer any distinctions between different peoples. In the church of Jesus Christ Jews and non-Jews are bound together in the name of Jesus. The "dividing wall" has been broken down (Eph. 2:11–22).

Does this mean, then, that we can safely ignore most of Leviticus? That would not be wise, for the church still has much to learn from these passages. We need to understand, for example, that God is a God of wholeness, holiness, and life. As those who love God, we need to learn how to reflect his holiness in our lives. This call to godliness, which is at the heart of these laws, will never change or become obsolete.

Perfect

In his life and words, Jesus emphasized the essence of the law time and again. In the Sermon on the Mount in Matthew 5–7, for example, we see that if someone does not actually kill another person, but scolds that person, the law has still been broken. If someone looks at a woman lustfully, this is the same as actually committing adultery. To truly live according to God's will requires treating others in a loving way. This means going one step further than expected in caring for each other. It also means keeping away from anything that may cause us to sin. In Matthew 15:10–20, Jesus says that uncleanness comes from the sinful things that live in our own hearts. Following rules about cleanness and uncleanness without inner purity does not make sense.

In Matthew 5:48, Jesus commands his followers: "Be perfect, therefore, as your heavenly Father is perfect." These words are almost the same as those in Leviticus 19:2: "Be holy because I, the LORD your God, am holy." God is the Holy One, without sin, and Israel was separated from others in order to serve him. They had to be committed to him wholeheartedly, or "perfectly." The Hebrew word for perfect is *tamim*, and it comes from a verb meaning "to be whole," "to be perfect." Jesus asks his disciples to be wholly committed to God and to his Kingdom with an undivided heart. That requires so much more than simply "not doing what the Ten Commandments forbid to do." John Colwell remarks on this verse:

> Jesus' concern here is not so much to give a new law as to reinterpret the old law, or rather, to indicate that which always was underlying the law – that we should live in coherence with the character of God . . .[143]

That Jesus longs for his disciples to be God's children with undivided hearts is also clear from his words in Matthew 6:24: "No one can serve two masters. Either he will hate the one and love the other, or he will be devoted to the one and despise the other. You cannot serve both God and Money."

In the Sermon on the Mount Jesus more than once addresses the issue of being a "whole" person. He reacts against hypocrisy, "speaking in two different ways," doing "as if." A disciple should be wholeheartedly and honestly committed to God's Kingdom. That comes first . . . "seek first his kingdom and his righteousness . . ." (Matt. 6:33).

I once heard David Wenham speak about the issue of clean and unclean food and how Jesus applied the laws regarding them in his life. We read in Mark 7:14–23 that Jesus declares all food clean. But that is not the only thing he does. He also breaks through the barriers of uncleanness and sin in this world by the way he lives. He has contacts with people who are "unclean" according to the rules of the time. Jesus does not abrogate the law of Moses, but he himself brings cleanness and purity to the people. God's desire that we should be "clean" and "whole" is not out of date – rather, it is fully realized in the life of Jesus. Jesus heals the sick, the "unclean," he touches the leper. He heals a woman who has lost blood for many years and who consequently is unclean. He brings all of these people back into the community of God. Jesus' holiness is so powerful that he even raises people from the dead. He does not become unclean through touching these people – rather, they become clean through their contact with him! His holiness, purity, and cleanness are "contagious," so to speak. Wenham described the situation of the New Testament as follows:

> God's concern for purity and wholeness is not diminished, but we are now in the age of redemption when God is intervening in Jesus to establish that wholeness.[144]

Everyone who is in Christ is now called "holy." In his first letter, Peter describes the Christian church in the same way as the Torah, and in particular Leviticus, describe the Old Testament people of God. Peter writes: "But you are a chosen people, a royal priesthood, a holy nation, a people belonging to God." The Christian church is chosen for a particular purpose: ". . . that you may declare the praises of him who called you out of darkness into his wonderful light" (1 Pet. 2:9).

In Ephesians 1:4 we read: "For he chose us in him before the creation of the world to be holy and blameless in his sight." Clearly God's grace comes first – just as we observed with regard to the Ten Commandments. He asks those whom he loves first to love and serve him wholeheartedly.

Wright's triangle

In Wright's triangle we saw Israel in the wider context of the broken world in which they were a paradigm, a sort of model. Wright also draws several lines from the Old Testament to the New. Some elements of the Old Testament, such as sacrifices and priesthood, typologically refer forward to spiritual realities in the New Testament. The idea of paradigm is still relevant for today's church, because we live in the context of a broken world and a fallen creation. The Christian church is meant to show what God's world could look like. By doing this, she also points forward to the future, to the "eschaton," when creation will be new and restored.[145]

The church, however, does not have a land of its own. Wright therefore replaces the word "land" in the triangle with the word *koinonia*, or "fellowship." The Christian community is meant to be a fellowship in the spiritual sense, but also in the practical sense. I do not agree with Wright when he substitutes "land" with the idea of *koinonia*. If the "land" is the realm where God's blessings are enjoyed and shared, and where we see his rules put into practice, is it not better to put "the Kingdom of God" in the place of the land in the triangle?[146] The Kingdom of God is everywhere where God is honored as King. The Sermon on the Mount shows what life in the Kingdom should look like – how practical the love for our sisters and brothers should be, how we should give to the needy and forgive others.

Wright has made a very valuable contribution to our thinking on the subject, however. According to Wright, for example, the food laws have a typological function in that they are "typical" of the wholeness, integrity, and holiness God requires in his people – most clearly visible in Jesus Christ.

The paradigmatic function of the food laws is clear: Israel stood out in the world as a people with a difference, even in their food. These laws have an eschatological function as well because they point to a "whole," "clean" world without blame or sin which in the future will become a reality. That ideal remains – even when the food laws in their literal sense no longer apply to the church. There will be a new heaven and a new earth and God will create a new Jerusalem of which it is said that nothing "impure will ever enter it . . ." (Rev. 21:27).

Cancellation of debts

As we have seen, Deuteronomy 15:1–11 presents a system for canceling debts that gave people a chance to start afresh every seventh year. God's desire was that each member of the covenant people would have a share in the promised land he had given them. This particular law also made clear that lending to a poor brother had to be done wholeheartedly – even with no expectation of being repaid. The Israelites were required to be open-minded and kind to their fellow-Israelites.

From the point of view of the New Testament, we can apply these rules today in several ways. First we need to think of "giving" and "forgiving" in the wider sense of these words. We need to do both wholeheartedly. Indeed, the way that Jesus describes the need for mutual forgiveness is as wholehearted as Deuteronomy. He challenges his disciples to forgive "seventy-seven times" (Matt. 18:22), which means an infinite number of times. Jesus also urges his disciples to be openhanded in giving to others: "Give to the one who asks you, and do not turn away from the one who wants to borrow from you" (Matt. 5:42). These are words from the Sermon on the Mount, which also contains many other practical guidelines for a life of discipleship. Jesus spoke these words in the context of the occupation of the land by the Romans, who could force Israelites at random to "go one mile" for them, carrying their burdens (v. 41). Jesus urges those who follow him to do more than is required or expected and to show abundant love – even to their enemies.

In the same vein, in Luke 6:34–36 we read:

> And if you lend to those from whom you expect repayment, what credit is that to you? Even "sinners" lend to "sinners," expecting to be repaid in full. But love your enemies, do good to them, and lend to them without expecting to get anything back. Then your reward will be great, and you will be sons of the Most High, because he is kind to the ungrateful and wicked. Be merciful, just as your Father is merciful.

These words remind us of several passages from Deuteronomy and Leviticus that we saw above. While Deuteronomy speaks mainly about giving to sisters and brothers, "love your neighbor as yourself" (Lev. 19:18) is a command that assumes we are not restricting our love to just a few friends or relatives. The other striking correspondence between the Old and New Testaments in the area of forgiveness is the way the disciples are to "reflect" the Father's mercy – just as the Israelites had to be "holy" even as God is holy. Jesus expects his followers to be as gracious and kind as God is – even to sinners. This requirement applies to giving all sorts of practical help, but also to forgiving.

The book of Acts, in describing the activities of the early church, gives us a glimpse of what it means to live as a new community in Christ, as the people of God. The community of believers reflects the "ideal" of Deuteronomy 15: providing a place in this broken world where people share not just their faith, but also their earthly goods. Acts 4:34, "There were no needy persons among them," echoes the command from Deuteronomy

15:4, ". . . there should be no poor among you."[147] The believers shared what they had and what they were: "All the believers were one in heart and mind. No one claimed that any of his possessions was his own, but they shared everything they had" (Acts 4:32). The result was that the church grew daily, because of the testimony given in word and in deed. The early church was indeed a "paradigm" of God's love and grace in a broken world.

The New Testament letters to the early churches are full of examples of believers giving and helping each other in practical ways. The words of the apostle Paul in 2 Corinthians 8 and 9 on this subject should be read in their entirety. To quote just one verse, ". . . God loves a cheerful giver' (2 Cor. 9:7). In Acts 20:35 Paul quotes some of Jesus' words that are not found anywhere else: "It is more blessed to give than to receive."

The other application of Deuteronomy 15, which we may call a "typological" one, is in the area of forgiveness. The New Testament letters also frequently address this issue. So, for example, Ephesians 4:32 says: "Be kind and compassionate to one another, forgiving each other, just as in Christ God forgave you." Similarly, Colossians 3:13 says: "Bear with each other and forgive whatever grievances you may have against one another. Forgive as the Lord forgave you." Both verses clearly establish the relationship between the grace given to us by God and the way in which we should treat others graciously. Because we are forgiven, we should forgive others. We affirm this truth every time we repeat the Lord's Prayer: "as we forgive those . . ." We can also see this principle at work in the parable of the king and his slaves in Matthew 18:23–35. In the Old Testament laws we saw exactly the same sort of relationship between God's conduct and ours. Because the Israelites knew what it meant to be aliens, they had to treat aliens gently and, in behaving like this, they would reflect God's character. Because Christians know what it is to be forgiven, they should forgive others, and in this way they will show something of the Father's character.[148]

Laws on warfare

When considering the New Testament application of the Old Testament laws on warfare, we should keep in mind one fundamental difference between the Old Testament people of Israel and the New Testament church. The followers of Jesus do not form a political entity; they do not own one land; nor are they restricted to one nation or ethnicity. The followers of Jesus Christ do not fight battles with human armies. Jesus said to Pilate: "My kingdom is not of this world. If it were, my servants would fight to prevent my arrest by the Jews. But now my kingdom is from another place" (John 18:36). "Christian" nations are not following these words when they wage war "in the name of God."

On another level, however, there is an ongoing battle in which all Christians must engage. Jesus prepared his disciples for this battle when he explained that their choice to follow him would result in animosity and resistance from those who would not believe in him. Even families may be divided because of him. When sending his disciples on their first missionary trip, Jesus said:

> I am sending you out like sheep among wolves. . . . Be on your guard against men; they will hand you over to the local councils and flog you in their synagogues. . . . All men will hate you because of me . . . (Matt. 10:16–17, 22)

The New Testament repeatedly reminds Christians that they have to suffer because of Jesus and that the battle

between him and the adversary cannot be won with
earthly weapons. 1 Peter contains an especially illuminating discussion of the sheer necessity of suffering for
Christians. Behind the animosity against Jesus' followers there is a spiritual battle going on, as we read in
Ephesians 6:10–19. Verses 11 and 12 tell us:

> Put on the full armor of God so that you can take your
> stand against the devil's schemes. For our struggle is not
> against flesh and blood, but against the rulers, against the
> authorities, against the powers of this dark world and
> against the spiritual forces of evil in the heavenly realms.

The "armor" that Paul describes in some detail does not
consist of guns, knives or weapons of mass destruction,
but rather of truth, righteousness, the gospel of peace,
faith, salvation, the word of God and prayer. These are
the "weapons" of God and his Kingdom, to be used by
his followers to conquer sin, injustice, and everything
that threatens to destroy life as he intended it.

Clear away

The battle between God and his adversary is not only
fought against outside forces; it is more than govern-
ments or individuals chasing after Christians. It is also a
battle within ourselves against everything which is con-
tradictory to God's will. Referring to the battle in our
own hearts and lives, Jesus speaks some very radical
words (again, in the Sermon on the Mount):

> If your right eye causes you to sin, gouge it out and throw
> it away. It is better for you to lose one part of your body
> than for your whole body to be thrown into hell. And if

your right hand causes you to sin, cut it off and throw it away. It is better for you to lose one part of your body than for your whole body to go into hell. (Matt. 5:29–30; see also 18:8–9; Mark 9:43–48)

We should immediately remove from our lives anything that might lead us to sin. A match should be extinguished before it causes a fire. In Matthew 5:21–22 and 27–28 Jesus argues that murder starts with scolding your "brother" and adultery with looking lustfully at a woman. He urges his followers, therefore, to put away everything that may cause them to be drawn away from him. Only by exercising this sort of vigilance will we be able to commit ourselves totally to God.

Paul says that even believers who continue to sin can be stumbling blocks and need to be removed from our presence: "Expel the wicked man from among you" (1 Cor. 5:13). All of this is in accordance with the principle we saw in Deuteronomy 20: Israel had to destroy whatever would lead them away from God and into sin. It was a matter of life (as the people of God) or death. Both the Old and the New Testaments urge those who love God to love him wholeheartedly and to do away with anything that is against his will.

Tremper Longman and Daniel Reid argue more or less along the same lines. They provide the following schedule for the biblical history: the Bible begins with "Eden" in Genesis and ends with "Eden restored" in the book of Revelation. They see the following five stage in between:

1. God fights Israel's enemies of flesh and blood.
2. God fights against Israel in judgement because of their sin.
3. The Old Testament prophets look forward to the day of God's deliverance.

4. Christ's first coming to the earth means that there is a battle between him and the spiritual powers.
5. At Christ's second coming, there will be a last, decisive battle, after which the situation of paradise will be restored.[149]

Wright's triangle clearly shows the paradigmatic element in the way that Israel had to deal with matters of war and warfare. In so far as we are involved in politics, we can certainly learn from the Old Testament – for example, in the area of ecological issues in warfare. The connection with the New Testament, however, is a typological one. The battle between God and his enemies continues from the Old Testament into the New. His power is much greater than that of his adversaries. While the idea of battle is present in the New Testament, it is of a different order than that in the Old Testament. Throughout both Testaments, however, it is God who can be trusted to gain victory. Seen from God's perspective, human powers are relative.

There is also an eschatological element in the battle, which becomes very clear in the book of Revelation. At the end of time the battle between Christ and his adversary will become fiercer still. God is often called "King" in Revelation, and the struggle is between his realm and that of Satan. The book of Revelation primarily uses the vocabulary of the Old Testament to describe this battle – for instance in chapters 17–18, which deal with the pride of Babylon, the great enemy of God and his Kingdom. There is a war between those belonging to Babylon and those belonging to Christ: "They will make war against the Lamb, but the Lamb will overcome them because he is Lord of lords and King of kings – and with him will be his called, chosen and faithful followers" (Rev. 17:14).

Finally, everything that is against God will be destroyed and God will be King forever. Those who love him will reign with him: "No longer will there be any curse. The throne of God and of the Lamb will be in the city, and his servants will serve him. . . . And they will reign for ever and ever" (Rev. 22:3, 5).

Towards an ethics of the Old and the New Testaments

Let us look finally at the characteristics of ethics we dealt with at the end of Chapter 6. Can they be applied to the Christian church?

1. We have seen that Old Testament ethics is based on God's grace. God saved Israel from Egypt, and the proper response to God's grace would be for Israel to obey his commands in thankfulness. Israel does not *become* God's people by obeying his commandments, but through obedience they show the reality of *being* the people of God. The same is true of the Christian church. Followers of Jesus have been saved by his blood, which he shed on the cross to reconcile us with God. Consequently, they show their love for him by obeying his commands. Through their lives they give an answer to his love and to God's grace. In 1 John 4:10 we read: "This is love: not that we loved God, but that he loved us and sent his Son as an atoning sacrifice for our sins." A command follows, which is more or less a "logical" result of this statement: "Dear friends, since God so loved us, we also ought to love one another" (v. 11).

The New Testament letters to Christians give rules for living *because* the readers now belong to Christ. They

have been saved by him and now ought to live according to that new status. In Paul's letter to the Colossians,
for instance, we read how the Christians in Colosse got
to know Jesus Christ: "For he has rescued us from the
dominion of darkness and brought us into the kingdom
of the Son he loves, in whom we have redemption, the
forgiveness of sins" (1:13). Christ "has rescued" us and
"brought" us into his Kingdom. At the point at which
someone comes to believe in him, this has already happened. In Colossians 2:6 Paul talks about the consequences for how each believer should live: "So then, just
as you received Christ Jesus as Lord, continue to live in
him . . ." We may say: "Become what you are in principle"; "Live according to your new nature."

The third chapter of Colossians begins with a similar
remark about the certainty of the new life that we now
have in Christ. Therefore, Paul argues, live according to
this new life – live as people from "above" (Col. 3:1). He
then goes on to elaborate how this new life becomes visible. First there is a list of things Christians should no
longer do (vv. 5–9), followed by a list of things which
belong to the new life of a Christian (vv. 12–17). The
words "chosen people," "holy" and "dearly loved" in
verse 12 remind us of the people of Israel who were
meant to live as the "people of God."

2. This brings us to the next point: Israel was supposed
   to be a paradigm in this broken world, and the same
   is true of the followers of Jesus. In Matthew 5:13–16
   Jesus says to his disciples:

You are the salt of the earth . . . You are the light of the
world. A city on a hill cannot be hidden. . . . In the same
way, let your light shine before men, that they may see your
good deeds and praise your Father in heaven.

Jesus' followers do not live separated from this world; yet they are different and should be distinct from other people so that they can be as visible as light and as noticeable as salt. Their words and actions should reveal to others something of the character of God the Father in heaven. Christians are God's representatives on earth – the purpose for which he created human beings in his own image (cf. Gen. 1:27).

In the early days of the church, Christians had a very clear paradigmatic function. We read in the book of Acts that those who did not yet believe in Jesus were attracted to the church, for Christians were "enjoying the favor of all the people. And the Lord added to their number daily those who were being saved" (Acts 2:47). The church was an "attractive" church, yet it was the Lord who added to their number. As paradigms we are not trying to draw attention to ourselves, but to point others to Jesus Christ.

The way in which Christians care for each other is still a paradigm in this world. Non-Christians are not attracted to a community of quarreling believers. Where love is invisible, it is hard to believe that God is Love. When we look back over the church's history, we must confess that the Christian church has often been a "negative" paradigm. Yet our challenge today remains the same: we need to study and follow Jesus' words and the example of the early church.

As we saw in Colossians 3 (see also Col. 4), Paul gives a picture of what a Christian should look like. It is all about reflecting what God has done for us: we are "dearly loved" and should therefore show kindness and compassion; we should forgive as the Lord forgave us (Col. 3:12–13). Philippians 2:14–15 emphasizes the paradigmatic function of the church as follows:

> Do everything without complaining or arguing, so that you
> may become blameless and pure, children of God without
> fault in a crooked and depraved generation, in which you
> shine like stars in the universe . . .

The words "blameless and pure" and "without fault"
remind us of the regulations in Leviticus concerning
priests, but also of the food laws and what is declared
clean by God. In the Old and New Testaments God's
ideal of wholeness and holiness, life and purity becomes
clear, as it is illustrated in Jesus' words to his disciples:
"Be perfect, therefore, as your heavenly Father is perfect" (Matt. 5:48).

The "paradigmatic" approach has been a fruitful way
of reading difficult texts such as the food laws and the
laws on warfare in the Old Testament. Does this mean
that the whole of Scripture could and should be read in
a paradigmatic way, as Birch and Rasmussen argue?[150]

Janzen seems to take a different approach. In the final
chapter of his *Old Testament Ethics* he argues that we
should see Jesus as our paradigm: as Priest, as Sage, as
King, as Prophet. He discusses passages in the New
Testament that testify to the uniqueness of the person of
Jesus, such as his priestly function in reconciling God
and humankind.[151] Birch and Rasmussen, on the other
hand, in paying more attention to Jesus as an example
for our conduct, are in danger of minimizing his uniqueness.

Janzen has interesting things to say about the "familial paradigm" and "life, land and hospitality" in Jesus'
life and in the New Testament church. Jesus invites
people to a banquet (Matt. 22:1–14; Luke 14:15–24), he
feeds five thousand people and he holds a Last Supper
with his disciples. Hospitality was likewise very important in the early church (Heb. 13:2); the fellowship at the

table of the Lord was essential in the Christian community.[152]

In general, I would argue that we cannot read the whole Bible in a paradigmatic way. People may be inspired by reading about "good behavior" in the Bible, but that is only part of the picture. Many people do good things because they are inspired by Jesus' example of care for the poor and the sick, but that does not make them followers of Jesus. Jesus Christ has done things that are impossible for any human being to do: he reconciled humanity with God by his death on the cross. He is able to forgive sins. He rose from the dead and has conquered sin and Satan. These facts are the foundation of our salvation and it is only by accepting them as true in our own lives that we become Christians. They are basic to the Christian life. Followers of Jesus may have to suffer in this world, but no sins are forgiven through their suffering, as through Jesus' suffering.

Jesus Christ can only become a real and enduring source of inspiration for our lives if he changes our hearts, if he becomes King in our lives. It is by the grace of God that we are changed into human beings who wish to do God's will wholeheartedly. It is the Holy Spirit who changes us from within, so that we can live as new beings, full of love, just as God intended humans to be from the beginning. By reading and studying Jesus' words Christians will, again and again, learn new insights for their own lives and for those of fellow Christians, as well as for living in this world.

3. Ethics in the Old Testament is "theocentric." The commands are good for the life of the people of Israel because they are God's commands. In the New Testament, too, there is a clear relationship between God and his commands. Often Jesus speaks about

doing the will of his "Father in heaven" (see again the
Sermon on the Mount). Those who love Christ keep
his commandments (John 14:21; 15:10).

4. There is no strict separation or division between
"spiritual" and "practical" laws – we cannot divide
our lives that way. What is the evidence that someone believes? Their words and actions make their
beliefs clear. In his letter James makes this issue clear
to his readers, but in actual fact Paul does the same –
by giving commands regarding how to live by faith.
A clear example of this is Romans 12–14, where we
find many commands concerning God, our "brothers and sisters," and our conduct in the non-
Christian world. There should be no discrepancy
between how we worship on Sundays and who we
are on Mondays.

5. Ethics is therefore a "way of life," the essence of which
is living in the presence of God. God's laws in the Old
Testament concern all of life, in all its facets. The same
is true of the commands in the New Testament.

6. The land played an important role in Israel's laws.
The land is the context in which Israel was to live as a
paradigm as the people of God in this world. We can,
as we saw above, replace "the land" in Wright's triangle with "the Kingdom of God." That Kingdom is not
of this earth – it is not a political entity with an
earthly king and an army. It is only partially visible.
We keep praying: "Thy kingdom come. . ." The followers of Jesus live in the period of God's history of
salvation in which this Kingdom has "already" come
in Jesus Christ, but is "not yet" fully revealed. Still,
their commission is to make God's presence and
Kingship visible on earth through their words and
deeds. Jesus gives the constitution of this Kingdom in
the Sermon on the Mount.

7. Ethics in the Old Testament was very much community-based. The lives and actions of individual Israelites were inextricably connected to the whole community. The people of God lived together as one body, united in the covenant. The situation is the same for the church and the believer in the New Testament, however. Birch and Rasmussen describe both Israel and the Christian church as follows: "The ethics were, to use the New Testament term, *koinonia*-ethics – community-creating human relatedness in a compelling experience of God."[153]

Paul further explores the close relationship between individual and community in the Christian church. In 1 Corinthians 12 he speaks about the Christian church as "one body." Christians are related to each other, just like the different parts of one body, through faith in one Lord. Believers have all received gifts from the Holy Spirit. Together they form a whole. The concept of one body and different parts reminds us of the idea of "corporate solidarity" in the Old Testament. Basically, Israel was one people because of the covenant at Sinai. In the same way, Christians are one people because of the new covenant in Christ. Paul wrote about the implications of the church's unity for its life together: "If one part suffers, every part suffers with it; if one part is honored, every part rejoices with it" (1 Cor. 12:26). This is, in fact, corporate solidarity.

Being one body is essential to the church, as its unity is not based on ethnicity or cultural circumstances. The foundation of the mutual solidarity of Christians is the personal relationship of each member with Christ. Geoffrey Grogan also expresses this conviction. He argues that the Letter to the Hebrews, like the rest of the New Testament, makes clear that in Jesus Christ a new community has been born, in which solidarity is shown in the same way as in the Old Testament: ". . . Christians are shown not simply to have an individual relationship with God, but membership in a community with as much sense of common interests as was the case in Old Testament days."[154]

There is much about the love of God and our love towards each other in 1 John. Christians are often commanded to love their "brother," which reminds us of the language of Deuteronomy 15:1–11.

What about solidarity within the family, or the clan, which was so important in Old Testament times? In the New Testament, fellowship with our "natural" family is subordinate to the relationship we have with Christ and with our "brothers and sisters" in the Christian church (see, e.g., Mark 3:31–35). People who are not part of our family, or who may not have relatives on earth at all, therefore have their own place within the family of God. Those who have lost their family because of their relationship with Jesus Christ receive a new family in their brothers and sisters in Christ (see Mark 10:29–30).

In Western society, where the individual is so central, the Christian church emphasizes that individuals are important to God, but that he binds them together into a loving and caring community. The Christian church should value the individual but not promote individualism, which is a negative trend in Western society because it threatens to destroy relationships. The church is meant to be a paradigm in society – as we show God's love and care for each other and, of course, for those outside as well, since every human being is created "in the image of God."[155] The church is supposed to show God's ideal for this world, which will one day be fully realized.

In everything, Christians and the Christian church live by God's grace in Jesus Christ, who was and is

God's greatest paradigm in this world. He showed God's ideal for humankind and for this world in his own person and life, in all that he did and said. That is why his followers may ask, time and again, in all circumstances: "What would Jesus do?"

Questions for further reflection

1. What are the particular areas in which you think the church's conduct can be paradigmatic for society?
2. The book of Acts tells us that the early Christians were "in favor with all the people." Does this mean that the church should be popular? Why or why not?
3. Why is it that Christians should expect persecution? What, if any, "persecution" have you suffered and what has it taught you?
4. Why is Jesus our model?
5. How can the certain outcome of the battle, as described in the book of Revelation, influence your life or the life of the church now?

Bibliography

Alexander, T. D., "Royal Expectations in Genesis to Kings: Their Importance for Biblical Theology," *Tyndale Bulletin* 49 (1998), 191–212.

Andersen, F. I., and D. N. Freedman, *Hosea* (Anchor Bible; New York: Doubleday, 1980).

Bahnsen, G. L., *Theonomy in Christian Ethics* (Nutley, NJ: Craig Press, 1977).

—— *No Other Standard: Theonomy and Its Critics* (Tyler, TX: Institute for Christian Economics, 1991).

Baker, D. L., *Two Testaments, One Bible: A Study of Some Modern Solutions to the Theological Problem of the Relationship between the Old and New Testaments* (Downers Grove, IL: InterVarsity Press, 1977).

Barton, J., "Understanding Old Testament Ethics," *Journal for the Study of the Old Testament* 9 (1978), 44–64.

—— "Approaches to Ethics in the Old Testament," in *Beginning Old Testament Study* (ed. J. Rogerson; London: SPCK, 1983), 113–30.

—— *Reading the Old Testament: Method in Biblical Study* (London: Darton, Longman & Todd, 2nd ed., 1996).

—— *Ethics and the Old Testament* (London: SCM Press, 2nd ed., 2002).

Berkhof, L., *Systematic Theology* (Grand Rapids: Eerdmans, 1939).

Birch, B. C., "Old Testament Narrative and Moral Address," in *Canon, Theology, and Old Testament Interpretation: Essays in Honor of B. S. Childs* (ed. G. M. Tucker, D. L. Petersen, and R. R. Wilson; Philadelphia: Fortress Press, 1988), 75–91.

—— *Let Justice Roll Down: The Old Testament, Ethics, and Christian Life* (Louisville: Westminster/John Knox Press, 1991).

—— and L. L. Rasmussen, *Bible and Ethics in the Christian Life* (Minneapolis: Augsburg, rev. ed., 1989).

Boecker, H. J., *Law and the Administration of Justice in the Old Testament and Ancient East* (London: SPCK, 1980).

Carmichael, C. M., "Forbidden Mixtures," *Vetus Testamentum* 32 (1982), 394–415.

—— *Law and Narrative in the Bible: The Evidence of the Deuteronomic Laws and the Decalogue* (Ithaca and London: Cornell University Press, 1985).

—— *The Spirit of Biblical Law* (Athens and London: University of Georgia Press, 1996).

Chave, C. B. (trans.), *The Commandments: Sefer Ha-Mitzvoth of Maimonides*, II (London: The Soncino Press, 1967).

Childs, B. S., *Introduction to the Old Testament as Scripture* (London: SCM Press, 1979).

—— *Old Testament Theology in a Canonical Context* (London: SCM Press, 1985).

Chirichigno, G. C., *Debt-Slavery in Israel and the Ancient Near East* (Journal for the Study of the Old Testament: Supplement Series 141; Sheffield: Sheffield Academic Press, 1993).

Colwell, J. E., *Living the Christian Story: The Distinctiveness of Christian Ethics* (Edinburgh and New York: T. & T. Clark, 2001).

Craigie, P. C., *The Problem of War in the Old Testament* (Grand Rapids: Eerdmans, 1978).

Darby, J. N., *The Hopes of the Church of God* (London: Francis Baisler, 2nd ed., 1842).

Douglas, M., *Purity and Danger: An Analysis of Concepts of Pollution and Taboo* (London: Routledge & Kegan Paul, 2nd ed., 1969).

—— *Leviticus as Literature* (Oxford: Oxford University Press, 1999).

Dumbrell, W. J., *Covenant and Creation: A Theology of the Old Testament Covenants* (Carlisle: Paternoster; Grand Rapids: Baker, 1993).

Dyrness, W., *Themes in Old Testament Theology* (Downers Grove, IL: InterVarsity Press; Carlisle: Paternoster, 1977).

Epsztein, L., *Social Justice in the Ancient Near East and the People of the Bible* (London: SCM Press, 1986).

Falk, Z. W., *Hebrew Law in Biblical Times: An Introduction* (Provo, UT: Brigham Young University Press; Winona Lake: Eisenbrauns, 2001).

Firmage, E., "The Biblical Dietary Laws and the Concept of Holiness," in *Studies in the Pentateuch* (ed. J. A. Emerton; Supplements to Vetus Testamentum 41; Leiden: Brill, 1990), 177–208.

Fletcher, V. H., "The Shape of Old Testament Ethics," *Scottish Journal of Theology* 24 (1971), 47–73.

France, R. T., *Matthew* (Tyndale New Testament Commentaries; Leicester: Inter-Varsity Press;, Grand Rapids: Eerdmans, 1985).

Goetze, A., "Warfare in Asia Minor," *Iraq* 25 (1963), 124–30.

Goldingay, J., *Approaches to Old Testament Interpretation* (Issues in Contemporary Theology; Downers Grove, IL: InterVarsity Press, 1981).

—— *Models for Interpretation of Scripture* (Grand Rapids: Eerdmans; Carlisle: Paternoster, 1995).

Grayson, A. K., *Assyrian Royal Inscriptions* I, II (Wiesbaden: Harrassowitz, 1972, 1976).

—— "Assyrian Civilization," in *The Cambridge Ancient History* 3.2 (ed. J. Boardman; Cambridge: Cambridge University Press, 1991), 194–228.

Grogan, G. W., "The Old Testament Concept of Solidarity in Hebrews," *Tyndale Bulletin* 49 (1998), 159–73.

Harrison, R. K., *Leviticus* (Tyndale Commentary; Leicester: Inter-Varsity Press, 1980).

Hartley, J. E., *Leviticus* (Word Biblical Commentary; Dallas: Word, 1992).

Hasel, G. F., *Old Testament Theology: Basic Issues in the Current Debate* (Grand Rapids: Eerdmans, 4th ed., 1991).

Hermisson, H. J., "Jesus Christus als externe Mitte des Alten Testaments: Ein unzeitgemässes Votum zur Theologie des Alten Testaments," in *Jesus Christus als Mitte der Schrift: Studien zur Hermeneutik des Evangeliums* (ed. C. Landmesser, H. J. Eckstein, and H. Lichtenberger; Berlin and New York: W. de Gruyter, 1997), 199–233.

Hobbs, T. R., *A Time for War: A Study of Warfare in the Old Testament* (Wilmington, DE: Glazier, 1989).

Houston, W., *Purity and Monotheism: Clean and Unclean Animals in Biblical Law* (Journal for the Study of the Old Testament: Supplement Series 140; Sheffield: Academic Press, 1993).

Janzen, W., *Old Testament Ethics: A Paradigmatic Approach* (Louisville: Westminster/John Knox Press, 1994).

Jenson, P. P., *Graded Holiness: A Key to the Priestly Conception of the World* (Journal for the Study of the Old Testament: Supplement Series 106; Sheffield: Sheffield Academic Press, 1992).

Jones, D. R., *Jeremiah* (New Century Bible; Grand Rapids: Eerdmans, 1992).

Joyce, P., "The Individual and the Community," in *Beginning Old Testament Study* (ed. J. Rogerson; London: SPCK, 1983), 74–89.

Kaiser, W. C., Jr., *Toward Old Testament Ethics* (Grand Rapids: Zondervan, 1983).

Kalluveettil, P., *Declaration and Covenant: A Comprehensive Review of Covenant Formulae from the Old Testament and the Ancient Near East* (Analecta biblica 88; Rome: Biblical Institute Press, 1982).

Kenyon, K. M., *Amorites and Canaanites* (Schweich Lectures 1963; London: Oxford University Press for the British Academy, 1966).

Korošec, V., "The Warfare of the Hittites – From the Legal Point of View," *Iraq* 25 (1963), 159–66.

Kuhn, T., *The Structure of Scientific Revolutions* (Chicago: University of Chicago Press, 2nd ed., 1970).

Lilley, J. P. U., "Understanding the Herem," *Tyndale Bulletin* 44 (1993), 169–77.

——— "The Judgement of God: The Problem of the Canaanites," *Themelios* 22.2 (1997), 3–12.

Lind, M. C., *Jahweh is a Warrior: The Theology of Warfare in Ancient Israel* (Scottdale, PA and Kitchener, ON: Herald Press, 1980).

Longman III, T., *Making Sense of the Old Testament: Three Crucial Questions* (Grand Rapids: Baker, 1998).

——— and D. G. Reid, *God is a Warrior* (Grand Rapids: Zondervan; Carlisle: Paternoster, 1995).

Mackintosh, C. H., *Notes on the Book of Leviticus* (London: Morrish, 1860).

Martens, E. A., *God's Design: A Focus on Old Testament Theology* (Grand Rapids: Baker Books, 2nd ed., 1994).

McConville, J. G., *Law and Theology in Deuteronomy* (Journal for the Study of the Old Testament: Supplement Series 33; Sheffield: JSOT Press, 1984).

—— *Grace in the End: A Study in Deuteronomic Theology* (Carlisle: Paternoster, 1993).

—— *Deuteronomy* (Apollos Old Testament Commentary; Leicester and Downers Grove, IL: Apollos, 2002).

Mendenhall, G. E., "Covenant Forms in Israelite Tradition," *Biblical Archaeologist* 17 (1954), 50–76.

—— *The Syllabic Inscriptions from Byblos* (Beirut: American University, 1985).

—— and G. A. Herion, "Covenant," *The Anchor Bible Dictionary*, I (ed. D. N. Freedman; New York: Doubleday, 1992), 1179–1202.

Milgrom, J., "The Biblical Diet Laws as an Ethical System," *Interpretation* 17 (1963), 288–301, also in *idem, Studies in Cultic Theology and Terminology* (Studies in Judaism in Late Antiquity 63; Leiden: E. J. Brill, 1983), 104–18.

—— *Leviticus 1–16* (Anchor Bible; New York: Doubleday, 1991).

Millar, J. G., "The Ethics of Deuteronomy: An Exegetical and Theological Study" (Dissertation Abstract), *Tyndale Bulletin* 46 (1995), 389–92.

—— *Now Choose Life: Theology and Ethics in Deuteronomy* (New Studies in Biblical Theology 6; Leicester: Apollos, 1998).

Millard, A., *Discoveries from Bible Times: Archaeological Treasures Throw Light on the Bible* (Oxford: Lion, 1997).

Mitchell, T. C., *The Bible in the British Museum* (London: British Museum Press, 1996).

Moor, J. C. de, *New Year with Canaanites and Israelites* (Kamper Cahiers 21 and 22; Kampen: Kok, 1972).

Niditch, S., *War in the Hebrew Bible: A Study in the Ethics of Violence* (New York and Oxford: Oxford University Press, 1993).

Noth, M., *Leviticus* (Old Testament Library; London: SCM Press, 1965).

Ogletree, T. W., *The Use of the Bible in Christian Ethics* (Oxford: Basil Blackwell, 1984).

Otto, E., *Theologische Ethik des Alten Testaments* (Stuttgart: Kohlhammer, 1994).

Paley, S. M., *King of the World: Ashur-nasir-pal II of Assyria 883–859 B.C.*. (New York: Brooklyn Museum, 1976).

Paul, S. M., *Studies in the Book of the Covenant in the Light of Cuneiform and Biblical Law* (Supplements to Vetus Testamentum XVIII; Leiden: Brill, 1970).

Peels, H. G. L., *Shadow Sides: God in the Old Testament* (Carlisle: Paternoster Press, 2003).

Porter, B. N., *Images, Power, and Politics: Figurative Aspects of Esarhaddon's Babylonian Policy* (Philadelphia: American Philosophical Society, 1993).

Pritchard, J. B., *Ancient Near Eastern Texts Relating to the Old Testament* (Princeton, NJ: Princeton University Press, 2nd ed., 1955).

Rad, G. von, *Holy War in Ancient Israel* (Grand Rapids: Eerdmans, 1991 [German 1958]).

—— *Old Testament Theology*, I (London: SCM Press, 1975 [German 1957]).

—— "The Problem of the Hexateuch," in *The Problem of the Hexateuch and Other Essays* (Edinburgh: Oliver & Boyd, 1966), 1–78.

Reade, J., *Assyrian Sculpture* (London: British Museum Press, 2nd ed., 1998).

Rendtorff, R., *The Problem of the Process of Transmission in the Pentateuch* (Journal for the Study of the Old Testament: Supplement Series 89; Sheffield: JSOT Press, 1990 [German 1977]).

—— "Is it Possible to Read Leviticus as a Separate Book?" in *Reading Leviticus: A Conversation with Mary Douglas* (ed. J. F. A. Sawyer; Journal for the Study of the Old Testament: Supplement Series 227; Sheffield: Academic Press, 1996), 22–35.

Robinson, H. W., *The Cross in the Old Testament* (London: SCM Press, 1955).

—— *The Christian Doctrine of Man* (Edinburgh: T. & T. Clark, 1911).

—— *Corporate Personality in Ancient Israel* (Philadelphia: Fortress Press, rev. ed., 1980).

Rodd, C. S., *Glimpses of a Strange Land: Studies in Old Testament Ethics* (Old Testament Studies; Edinburgh: T. & T. Clark, 2001).

—— "Old Testament Ethics," *Epworth Review* 30.2 (2003), 35–41.

Rofé, A., "The Laws of Warfare in the Book of Deuteronomy: Their Origins, Intent and Positivity," *Journal for the Study of the Old Testament* 32 (1985), 23–44.

—— "The Arrangement of the Laws in Deuteronomy," *Ephemerides Theologicae Lovanienses* 64 (1988), 265–87.

Rosner, B. S., "The Concept of Idolatry," *Themelios* 24.3 (1999), 23–24.

Roth, M., *Law Collections from Mesopotamia and Asia Minor* (Atlanta, GA: Scholars Press, 1995).

Ruler, A. A. van, *The Christian Church and the Old Testament* (trans. G. W. Bromiley; Grand Rapids: Eerdmans, 1971 [Dutch 1955]).

Saggs, H. W. F., "Assyrian Warfare in the Sargonid Period," *Iraq* 25 (1963), 145–54.

—— *The Might that Was Assyria* (London: Sidgwick & Jackson, 1984).

Saint-Laurent, G. E., "Light from Ras Shamra on Elijah's Ordeal upon Mount Carmel," in *Scripture in Context: Essays on the Comparative Method* (ed. C. D. Evans, W. W. Hallo, and J. B. White; Pittsburgh Theological Monograph Series 34; Pittsburgh: Pickwick Press, 1980), 123–39.

Soden, W. von, "Der Assyrer und der Krieg," *Iraq* 25 (1963), 131–44.

Staniforth, M. (trans.), *Early Christian Writings: The Apostolic Fathers* (Harmondsworth: Penguin Books, 1968).

Stott, J. R. W., *New Issues Facing Christians Today* (London: Marshall Pickering, rev. ed., 1999).

Thackeray, H. St. J. (trans.), *The Letter of Aristeas* (London and New York: SPCK, 1917).

Veenhof, K. R., "History of the Ancient Near East to the Time of Alexander the Great," in *The World of the Bible* (Bible Handbook, I; Grand Rapids: Eerdmans, 1986), 202–327.

Veijola, T., "Der Dekalog bei Luther und in der heutigen Wissenschaft," in *idem, The Law in the Bible and in its Environment* (Helsinki: Finnish Exegetical Society; Göttingen: Vandenhoeck & Ruprecht, 1990), 63–90.

Vriezen, Th. C., *An Outline of Old Testament Theology* (Oxford: Oxford University Press, 1958 [Dutch 1949]).

Weinfeld, M., "The Covenant of Grant in the Old Testament and in the Ancient Near East," *Journal of the American Oriental Society* 90 (1970), 184–203.

——— "Sabbatical Year and Jubilee in the Pentateuchal Laws and their Ancient Near Eastern Background," in T. Veijola, *The Law in the Bible and in its Environment* (Helsinki: Finnish Exegetical Society; Göttingen: Vandenhoeck & Ruprecht, 1990), 39–62.

―――― *Deuteronomy* (Anchor Bible; New York: Double-day, 1991).

Wenham, D., "Leviticus 11," *meditation at Wycliffe Hall, Oxford*, May 20, 1994 (unpublished).

Wenham, G. J., "Grace and Law in the Old Testament," in *Law, Morality and the Bible: A Symposium* (ed. B. N. Kaye and G. J. Wenham; Downers Grove, IL: InterVarsity Press, 1978), 3–23.

―――― "Law and the Legal System in the Old Testament," in *Law, Morality and the Bible: A Symposium* (ed. B. N. Kaye and G. J. Wenham; Downers Grove, IL: InterVarsity Press, 1978), 24–52.

―――― *The Book of Leviticus* (New International Commentary on the Old Testament; Grand Rapids: Eerdmans, 1979).

―――― *Genesis* 1–15 (Word Biblical Commentary; Waco: Word, 1987).

―――― *Story as Torah: Reading the Old Testament Ethically* (Edinburgh: T. &.T. Clark, 2000).

Wenham, J. W., *The Goodness of God* (London: Inter-Varsity Press, 1974).

Westermann, C., *Elements of Old Testament Theology* (trans. D. W. Stott; Atlanta: John Knox Press, 1982 [German 1978]).

Wilson, R. R., "Approaches to Old Testament Ethics," in *Canon, Theology, and Old Testament Interpretation: Essays in Honor of B. S. Childs* (ed. G. M. Tucker, D. L. Petersen, and R. R. Wilson; Philadelphia: Fortress Press, 1988), 62–74.

Wiseman, D. J., *The Vassal-Treaties of Esarhaddon* (London: British School of Archaeology, 1958 [= *Iraq* 20, 1958]).

Wright, C. J. H., *Living as the People of God: The Relevance of Old Testament Ethics* (Leicester: Inter-Varsity Press, 1983).

—— "What Happened Every Seven Years in Israel? Old Testament Sabbatical Institutions for Land, Debts and Slaves, Part II," *The Evangelical Quarterly* 56 (1984), 193–201.

—— "Ethical Decisions in the Old Testament" (paper for the Fellowship of European Evangelical Theologians, 1990, unpublished).

—— *God's People in God's Land: Family, Land, and Property in the Old Testament* (Grand Rapids: Eerdmans; Exeter: Paternoster, 1990).

—— "The People of God and the State in the Old Testament," *Themelios* 16.1 (1990), 4–10.

—— "The Ethical Authority of the Old Testament: A Survey of Approaches, Part 1," *Tyndale Bulletin* 43.1 (1992), 101–20; "Part 2," *Tyndale Bulletin* 43.2 (1992), 203–31.

—— *Walking in the Ways of the Lord: The Ethical Authority of the Old Testament* (Leicester: Apollos, 1995).

—— *Deuteronomy* (New International Biblical Commentary; Peabody, MA: Hendrickson, 1996).

Wright, D. P., "Unclean and Clean (Old Testament)," *The Anchor Bible Dictionary*, VI (ed. D. N. Freedman; New York: Doubleday, 1993), 729–41.

Yadin, Y., *The Art of Warfare in Biblical Lands in the Light of Archaeological Discovery* (London: Weidenfeld & Nicolson, 1963).

Zimmerli, W., *Old Testament Theology in Outline* (Edinburgh: T. & T. Clark, 1978).

Endnotes

[1] Hetty Lalleman-de Winkel, *Van Levensbelang: De Relevantie van de Oudtestamentische Ethiek* (Zoetermeer: Boekencentrum, 1999).

[2] See, e.g., L. Berkhof, *Systematic Theology* (Grand Rapids: Eerdmans, 1939), 14.

[3] C. J. H. Wright, *Walking in the Ways of the Lord: The Ethical Authority of the Old Testament* (Leicester: Apollos, 1995), 74–79. Wright deals extensively with several main opinions in the discussion of the ethical value of the Old Testament.

[4] See, e.g., G. L. Bahnsen, *Theonomy in Christian Ethics* (Nutley, NJ: Craig Press, 1977), and *No Other Standard: Theonomy and Its Critics* (Tyler, TX: Institute for Christian Economics, 1991).

[5] J. N. Darby, *The Hopes of the Church of God* (London: Francis Baisler, 2nd ed., 1842), 86.

[6] "Jehovah" is the name used for God in older translations. Today the form "Yahweh," or "Jahweh," is accepted as the best rendering of the Hebrew letters YHWH. Out of reverence, Jews do not pronounce this name.

[7] G. von Rad, "The Problem of the Hexateuch," in *The Problem of the Hexateuch and Other Essays* (Edinburgh: Oliver & Boyd, 1966), 1–78. See also von Rad's *Old Testament Theology*, I (London: SCM Press, 1975).

[8] C. Westermann, *Elements of Old Testament Theology* (Atlanta: John Knox Press, 1982), 178.

[9] Westermann, *Theology*, 178.

[10] Th. C. Vriezen, *An Outline of Old Testament Theology* (Oxford: OUP, 1958), 88–89.

[11] J ("Jahwist") is the source in which God is referred to as "Yahweh" (the LORD); E ("Elohist") is the source which calls God simply "God."

[12] See, e.g., the works of B. S. Childs, *Introduction to the Old Testament as Scripture* (London: SCM Press, 1979) and *Old Testament Theology in a Canonical Context* (London: SCM Press, 1985).

[13] A simple concentric form is A – B – C – B′ – A′. The words of A – B and of B′ – A′ surround C, which is the central event or thought of the passage.

[14] R. Rendtorff, "Is it Possible to Read Leviticus as a Separate Book?" in *Reading Leviticus: A Conversation with Mary Douglas* (ed. J. F. A. Sawyer; JSOTSup 227; Sheffield: Sheffield Academic Press, 1996), 34.

[15] For more on the importance of the Bible stories for conveying ethical principles, see G. J. Wenham, *Story as Torah: Reading the Old Testament Ethically* (Edinburgh: T. & T. Clark, 2000) and J. E. Colwell, *Living the Christian Story: The Distinctiveness of Christian Ethics* (Edinburgh and New York: T. & T. Clark, 2001).

[16] For a discussion see G. F. Hasel, *Old Testament Theology: Basic Issues in the Current Debate* (Grand Rapids: Eerdmans, 4th ed., 1991), chap. 4, "The Center of the OT and OT Theology."

[17] So E. A. Martens, *God's Design: A Focus on Old Testament Theology* (Grand Rapids: Baker Books, 2nd ed., 1994).

[18] See n. 5, above.

[19] Westermann, *Theology*.

[20] H. J. Hermisson, "Jesus Christus als externe Mitte des Alten Testaments: Ein unzeitgemässes Votum zur Theologie des Alten Testaments," in *Jesus Christus als Mitte der Schrift:*

Studien zur Hermeneutik des Evangeliums (ed. C. Landmesser, H. J. Eckstein, and H. Lichtenberger; Berlin and New York: W. de Gruyter, 1997), 199–233.

[21] See also Rev. 11:17–18.

[22] E. Otto, *Theologische Ethik des Alten Testaments* (Stuttgart: Kohlhammer, 1994), 92–94.

[23] Otto, *Ethik*, 94–99, discusses this psalm under the heading "The ethos which is theologically legitimized by creation."

[24] See, e.g., G. J. Wenham, *Genesis 1–15* (WBC; Waco: Word, 1987), 29–32.

[25] Wenham, *Story as Torah*, 25.

[26] For a more extensive exposition of the theology of Genesis and recurring themes in Genesis 1–11 and the rest of the book, see Wenham, *Story as Torah*, chap. 3.

[27] W. J. Dumbrell, *Covenant and Creation: A Theology of the Old Testament Covenants* (Carlisle: Paternoster; Grand Rapids: Baker, 1993), 62.

[28] Dumbrell, *Covenant*, 61.

[29] See Wenham, *Story as Torah*, chap. 3, for the overall structure of Genesis; also Dumbrell, *Covenant*, chap. 2.

[30] We will return to this battle in the final chapters.

[31] In the OT, chaos is the situation before creation when God brought order and life. Sin causes chaos to return again – it reverses the work of creation, so to speak, as we read in Jer. 4:23–26.

[32] See P. Kalluveettil, *Declaration and Covenant: A Comprehensive Review of Covenant Formulae from the Old Testament and the Ancient Near East* (AnBib 88; Rome: Pontifical Biblical Institute, 1982).

[33] G. E. Mendenhall, "Covenant Forms in Israelite Tradition," *BA* 17 (1954), 50–76; also G. E. Mendenhall and G. A. Herion, "Covenant," *ABD*, I (New York: Doubleday, 1992), 1179–1202.

[34] C. J. H. Wright, *Deuteronomy* (NIBC; Peabody, MA: Hendrickson, 1996), 3.

[35] Wenham, *Story as Torah*, 81–82.

[36] M. Weinfeld, "The Covenant of Grant in the Old Testament and in the Ancient Near East," *JAOS* 90 (1970), 184–203.

[37] Some commentators think that this text refers to the generation that was brought out of Egypt, but it seems more accurate to think of Abram, Isaac, and Jacob, as in Deut. 6:10.

[38] G. E. Mendenhall, *The Syllabic Inscriptions from Byblos* (Beirut: American University, 1985); also, with Herion, "Covenant."

[39] S. M. Paul, *Studies in the Book of the Covenant in the Light of Cuneiform and Biblical Law* (VTSup XVIII; Leiden: Brill, 1970), 30–31.

[40] Different scholars date the text differently.

[41] Paul, *Studies*, 5, 23.

[42] J. G. McConville, *Deuteronomy* (Leicester and Downers Grove, IL: Apollos, 2002), 34–35.

[43] Paul, *Studies*, 9.

[44] Z. W. Falk, *Hebrew Law in Biblical Times: An Introduction* (Provo, UT: Brigham Young University Press; Winona Lake: Eisenbrauns, 2001), 11, 5.

[45] L. Epsztein, *Social Justice in the Ancient Near East and the People of the Bible* (London: SCM Press, 1986), 105.

[46] Epsztein, *Social Justice*, 107.

[47] See Deut. 6:5. For an explanation of "holiness," see G. J. Wenham, *The Book of Leviticus* (NICOT; Grand Rapids: Eerdmans, 1979), 18–25.

[48] See p. 28.

[49] See Num. 27:1–11; Lev. 25:23–28; also Exod. 20:17: "You shall not covet . . . anything that belongs to your neighbor."

[50] W. C. Kaiser, Jr., *Toward Old Testament Ethics* (Grand Rapids: Zondervan, 1983).

[51] Kaiser, *Ethics*, chaps. 9–15 (pp. 139–244).

[52] Kaiser, *Ethics*, 63–64.

[53] Kaiser, *Ethics*, 312.

[54] Wenham, *Leviticus*, 32–33, argues that the division is arbitrary and only uses it with some reserve.

[55] W. Janzen, *Old Testament Ethics: A Paradigmatic Approach* (Louisville: Westminster/John Knox Press, 1994), 90.

[56] Janzen, *Ethics*, 92–95. Janzen also remarks that in the Sermon on the Mount Jesus did not deal with all the commandments of the Decalogue, but rather selected a few to give examples for the whole of life for his followers (95).

[57] Janzen, *Ethics*, 89.

[58] Janzen, *Ethics*, 55–58, 90.

[59] Janzen, *Ethics*, 28.

[60] Janzen, *Ethics*, p. 46 n. 4, and p. 101 n. 12, referring to Kaiser, *Ethics*, who regards the laws in the Pentateuch as the heart of Old Testament ethics without paying much attention to the Prophets and the Wisdom Literature.

[61] Janzen, *Ethics*, 74.

[62] Janzen, *Ethics*, 96–99.

[63] Janzen, *Ethics*, 40–44.

[64] J. Barton, "Approaches to Ethics in the Old Testament," in *Beginning Old Testament Study* (ed. J. Rogerson; London: SPCK, 1983), 128.

[65] C. J. H. Wright, *Living as the People of God: The Relevance of Old Testament Ethics* (Leicester: Inter-Varsity Press, 1983), 43; published in the US as *An Eye for an Eye: The Place of Old Testament Ethics Today* (Downers Grove, IL: IVP, 1983).

[66] T. Kuhn, *The Structure of Scientific Revolutions* (Chicago: University of Chicago Press, 2nd ed., 1970).

[67] Wright, *Walking*, 60.

[68] Wright, *Walking*, 63.

[68] See above. Janzen, *Ethics*, 27–28, criticizes *Living as the People of God*, but Wright later developed his definition of paradigm in *Walking in the Ways of the Lord*.

[70] Janzen, *Ethics*, 27–28.

[71] Janzen, *Ethics*, 28–29.

[72] Janzen, *Ethics*, 58.

[73] B. C. Birch, *Let Justice Roll Down: The Old Testament, Ethics, and Christian Life* (Louisville: Westminster/John Knox Press, 1991), e.g., 42–43.

[74] B. C. Birch and L. L. Rasmussen, *Bible and Ethics in the Christian Life* (Minneapolis: Augsburg, rev. ed., 1989), 144–58 and 190–91.

[75] C. S. Rodd, *Glimpses of a Strange Land* (Edinburgh: T. & T. Clark, 2001), 313.

[76] Rodd, *Glimpses*, 321.

[77] Rodd, *Glimpses*, 322.

[78] Rodd, *Glimpses*, 327.

[79] Wenham, *Story as Torah*, 80.

[80] See Wright, *Living*, mainly 9–64; Wright, *Walking*, 26–39.

[81] See Wright.

[82] Wright, *Living*, 29.

[83] Wright, *Living*, 89.

[84] Wright, *Living*, 90.

[85] Otto, *Ethik*, 10–11.

[86] See in particular Wright, *Walking*, part 3.

[87] In the New Testament that whole is primarily Jesus' family, the church.

[88] H. W. Robinson introduced the concept of "corporate personality" in *The Christian Doctrine of Man* (Edinburgh: T. & T. Clark, 1911) and *Corporate Personality in Ancient Israel* (Philadelphia: Fortress Press, rev. ed., 1980). He applied it in *The Cross in the Old Testament* (London: SCM Press, 1955). Others refer to the concept of "corporate solidarity." See also Kaiser, *Ethics*, 67–72. We recognize the Hebrew way of speech in the way we use the concept of the "unknown soldier": one person as a representative of all fallen soldiers. Also P. Joyce, "The Individual and the Community," in *Beginning Old Testament Study* (ed. J. Rogerson; London: SPCK, 1983), 74–89.

[89] Vriezen, *Theology*, 326.

[90] In the same way, the community of Christians in the New Testament has the same basis.

[91] W. Zimmerli, *Old Testament Theology in Outline* (Edinburgh: T. & T. Clark, 1978), 138–39.

[92] Martens, *God's Design*, 73.

[93] For a helpful division of the chapter, see Wenham, *Leviticus*, 165.

[94] Maimonides, *Moreh Nebuchim* 3.48, quoted in *The Commandments: Sefer Ha-Mitzvoth of Maimonides*, II (trans. C. B. Chave; London: The Soncino Press, 1967), 168.

[95] See R. K. Harrison, *Leviticus* (Tyndale Commentary; Leicester: Inter-Varsity Press, 1980).

[96] See M. Noth, *Leviticus* (OTL; London: SCM Press, 1965), 92.

[97] H. St. J. Thackeray (trans.), *The Letter of Aristeas* (London and New York: SPCK, 1917), par. 145–7, 150.

[98] The author was an unknown person who lived several generations after the biblical Barnabas; the epistle is therefore a pseudepigraph.

[99] M. Staniforth (trans.), "The Epistle of Barnabas," in *Early Christian Writings: The Apostolic Fathers* (Harmondsworth: Penguin Books, 1968), 187–222, par. 10.

[100] C. H. Mackintosh, *Notes on the Book of Leviticus* (London: Morrish, 1860), 189; see Chapter 1, above, on Darby and the Dispensationalist approach.

[101] J. Milgrom, *Leviticus 1–16* (AB; New York: Doubleday, 1991), 733–36; "The Biblical Diet Laws as an Ethical System," *Interpretation* 17 (1963), 288–301, and in *Studies in Cultic Theology and Terminology* (SJLA; Leiden: E. J. Brill, 1983), 104–18.

[102] For more on this concept of holiness see 6., below.

[103] E. Firmage, "The Biblical Dietary Laws and the Concept of Holiness," in *Studies in the Pentateuch* (ed. J. A. Emerton; VTSup 41; Leiden: E. J. Brill, 1990), 177–208.

[104] P. P. Jenson, *Graded Holiness: A Key to the Priestly Conception of the World* (JSOTSup 106; Sheffield: Sheffield Academic Press, 1992); W. Houston, *Purity and Monotheism: Clean and Unclean Animals in Biblical Law* (JSOTSup 140; Sheffield: Sheffield Academic Press, 1993).

[105] Wenham, *Leviticus*; J. E. Hartley, *Leviticus* (WBC; Dallas: Word, 1992).

[106] Wenham, *Story as Torah*, 134–43.

[107] M. Douglas, *Purity and Danger: An Analysis of Concepts of Pollution and Taboo* (London: Routledge & Kegan Paul, 2nd ed., 1969), esp. 41–57.

[108] Similarly Hartley, *Leviticus*, emphasizes the issue of life over against death.

[109] See B. S. Rosner, "The Concept of Idolatry," *Themelios* 24.3 (1999), 23–24.

[110] J. C. de Moor, *New Year with Canaanites and Israelites* (Kamper Cahiers 21–22; Kampen: Kok, 1972), vol. 21, pp. 6–8. The texts have been translated in vol. 22.

[111] F. I. Andersen and D. N. Freedman, *Hosea* (AB; New York: Doubleday, 1980), 157–58 state: "The perversion of sex, and an excessive preoccupation with it, are common factors in Canaanite religion and much ancient magic."

[112] Wenham, *Story as Torah*, 140.

[113] Wenham, *Story as Torah*, 137.

[114] Wenham, *Story as Torah*, 138.

[115] See Milgrom, *Leviticus*, 722–25, and esp. 731. See under 5., above, for other observations he makes.

[116] See Chapter 1, above, for a discussion of divisions the church has often made throughout its history.

[117] Discussed in the context of Lev. 19, above.

[118] In the Hebrew, the verbs for "lend" and "open" are both used twice to increase their impact. Cf. NKJV: "but you shall open your hand wide to him and willingly lend him sufficient for his need, whatever he needs."

[119] 2 Cor. 6:15 uses the name Belial to refer to Satan.

[120] Wenham, *Leviticus*, 322–23. It is not quite clear whether the command to free the slaves in Deut. 15:12–18 belongs to the Sabbath year, as the cancellation of debts does. Leviticus 25 deals with freeing slaves in the fiftieth year. Or does the latter passage apply to another group of slaves, who are

"Israelites of birth," whereas Deut. 15 (and Exod. 21:1–6) speak about "Hebrews," who may be a separate group of "outlaws" in society? That is what C. J. H. Wright suggests (*God's People in God's Land: Family, Land, and Property in the Old Testament* [Grand Rapids: Eerdmans; Exeter: Paternoster, 1990], 249–59; *Deuteronomy*, 197; "What Happened Every Seven Years in Israel? Old Testament Sabbatical Institutions for Land, Debts and Slaves, Part II," *EQ* 56 [1984], 193–201), but it is forcefully rejected by G. C. Chirichigno, *Debt-Slavery in Israel and the Ancient Near East* (JSOTSup 141; Sheffield: Sheffield Academic Press, 1993), 263–301.

[121] Law book of Hammurabi, par. 15 and 16.

[122] H. J. Boecker, *Law and the Administration of Justice in the Old Testament and Ancient East* (London: SPCK, 1980), 162.

[123] Boecker, *Law,* 163.

[124] See D. R. Jones, *Jeremiah* (New Century Bible; Grand Rapids: Eerdmans, 1992).

[125] Wenham, *Story as Torah,* 75.

[126] See A. Rofé, "The Laws of Warfare in the Book of Deuteronomy: Their Origins, Intent and Positivity," *JSOT* 32 (1985), 23–44. M. Weinfeld, *Deuteronomy* (AB; New York: Doubleday, 1991), 383–84, thinks there were different views on the relationship to the Canaanites. In the "Priestly" and "Deuteronomistic" sources, the extinction of the Canaanites was considered a task for the Israelites. This is not the case in the JE-source, where it is God who will drive the Canaanites out of the promised land.

[127] Like S. Niditch, *War in the Hebrew Bible: A Study in the Ethics of Violence* (New York and Oxford: OUP, 1993). She argues that there are six different opinions on warfare in the Old Testament, from writers who glorify war to the more pacifist ones.

[128] T. R. Hobbs, *A Time For War: A Study of Warfare in the Old Testament* (Wilmington, DE: Glazier, 1989), 226.

[129] Wright, *Deuteronomy,* 231.

[130] Based on conversations with the Assyriologists K. R. Veenhof (Leiden University) and A. R. Millard (University of Liverpool). Literature on the subject includes: K. R. Veenhof, "History of the Ancient Near East to the Time of Alexander the Great," in *The World of the Bible* (Bible Handbook, I; Grand Rapids: Eerdmans, 1986), 202–327; A. K. Grayson, "Assyrian Civilization," in *The Cambridge Ancient History* 3.2 (ed. J. Boardman; Cambridge: CUP, 1991), 194–228; A. Goetze, "Warfare in Asia Minor," *Iraq* 25 (1963), 124–30; W. von Soden, "Der Assyrer und der Krieg," *Iraq* 25 (1963), 131–44; H. W. F. Saggs, "Assyrian Warfare in the Sargonid Period," *Iraq* 25 (1963), 145–54; V. Korošec, "The Warfare of the Hittites – From the Legal Point of View," *Iraq* 25 (1963), 159–66; H. W. F. Saggs, *The Might that was Assyria* (London: Sidgwick & Jackson, 1984), 246–50.

[131] A good illustration of this rule is found in the story of Gideon (Judg. 7:3).

[132] Grayson, "Assyrian Civilization," 220.

[133] Y. Yadin, *The Art of Warfare in Biblical Lands in the Light of Archaeological Discovery* (London: Weidenfeld & Nicolson, 1963).

[134] See, e.g., the royal inscriptions of Ashur-nasir-pal II in S. M. Paley, *King of the World: Ashur-nasir-pal II of Assyeria 883–859 B.C.* (New York: Brooklyn Museum, 1976), 126–27, and those of Tiglath-Pileser in A. K. Grayson, *Assyrian Royal Inscriptions*, II (Wiesbaden: Harrassowitz, 1976), 6; also J. B. Pritchard, *Ancient Near Eastern Texts Relating to the Old Testament* (Princeton, NJ: Princeton University Press, 2nd ed., 1955). The material in the British Museum also testifies to the glorification of the king and his conquests.

[135] A. K. Grayson, *Assyrian Royal Inscriptions*, I (Wiesbaden: Harrassowitz, 1972), xx.

[136] Grayson, *Royal Inscriptions*, II, 6.

[137] McConville, *Deuteronomy*, 34.

[138] See M. C. Lind, *Jahweh is a Warrior: The Theology of Warfare in Ancient Israel* (Scottdale, PA and Kitchener, ON: Herald Press, 1980), esp. 156, 170–74.

[139] See Chapter 1, above.

[140] See Chapter 1, above.

[141] See D. L. Baker, *Two Testaments, One Bible: A Study of Some Modern Solutions to the Theological Problem of the Relationship between the Old and New Testaments* (Downers Grove, IL: IVP, 1977).

[142] A. A. van Ruler, *The Christian Church and the Old Testament* (Grand Rapids: Eerdmans, 1971).

[143] Colwell, *Living*, 112–13.

[144] Address in Wycliffe Hall, Oxford, May 20, 1994.

[145] Wright, *Walking*, 37–39; Wright, *Living*, 100.

[146] I think that there is yet a place for the people of Israel in their old land because God's promise to them has never been revoked. Of course that doesn't mean that everything Israel does as a political entity is right. Yet, with the Apostle Paul, I believe there is a future for Israel as a nation still.

[147] Wright makes this connection in *Living*, 101.

[148] The economic and political consequences of Deut. 15 are not dealt with here. Wright discusses several of these issues in *Walking in the Ways of the Lord*. He mentions the Jubilee Centre in Cambridge, England, which specifically deals with biblical concepts in politics. See also the reference to the London Institute for Contemporary Christianity, etc., in the Introduction, above.

[149] T. Longman III and D. G. Reid, *God is a Warrior* (Grand Rapids: Zondervan; Carlisle: Paternoster, 1995), 17.

[150] See Chapter 3, above.

[151] Janzen, *Ethics*, 193.

[152] Janzen, *Ethics*, 202–9.

[153] Birch and Rasmussen, *Bible and Ethics*, 31.

[154] G. W. Grogan, "The Old Testament Concept of Solidarity in Hebrews," *TynBul* 49 (1998), 159–73; quotation from p. 173.

[155] See Chapter 2, above.